DANCING OFF THE PAGE

Integrating performance, choreography, analysis and notation/documentation

DANCING OFF THE PAGE

Integrating performance, choreography, analysis and notation/documentation

Edited by
Rachel Duerden and Neil Fisher

With contributions by Jennifer Jackson, Bonnie Rowell
and Sarah Whatley, and music by Martin Blain

DANCE BOOKS

First published in 2007 by Dance Books Ltd
The Old Bakery
4 Lenten Street
Alton
Hampshire GU34 1HG

ISBN: 9 781852 731137

A CIP catalogue record for this book is available from the British Library

Printed and bound in Great Britain by Latimer Trend and Company Ltd, Plymouth, Devon

CONTENTS

Foreword

Dancing off the page incorporates new directions in the scholarly study of choreographic and performance style, and pedagogical research into the integration of theory and practice in dance studies. As such, it addresses itself both to the dance scholar and to the dance student.

Part 1 is a practical workbook, primarily for use in the studio. Notation is the unifying thread, extending into performance, choreography, documentation and critical analysis, and the book demonstrates how these strands can be effectively integrated in dance studies, in the studio as well as in the classroom or private study.

Part 2 includes three scholarly essays, each addressing key research issues that emerged in Part 1: philosophical issues in choreographic style and in performance style, and the nature of the relationship between performance, choreography and documentation.

Acknowledgements

The work for this project was supported by a Development Award from PALATINE, the Higher Education Academy Subject Centre for dance, drama and music.

The editors also gratefully acknowledge the support of Manchester Metropolitan University and Liverpool Institute of Performing Arts, and the contributions of students on the Dance Programme at MMU Cheshire who have trialled the material and offered valuable feedback and suggestions. Thanks are also due to Karolina Romaniszyn-Tong, who has given invaluable assistance in research, editing and the preparation of Labanotation scores.

Introduction

This book does two things in tandem: it explores notions of 'style' in dance performance and choreography, and it shows how the theory and practice of dance study can be successfully integrated, using notation as both a tool and a unifying factor. Part 1 explores these issues primarily in the context of practical dance experience in the studio. Part 2 explores issues in a more traditionally academic framework. The overarching aim is to demonstrate and illuminate the inter-relationship of these two approaches.

Notation as a means of recording and preserving dance is not as intimately connected with the *making* of dances, or choreography, as it is in music, for example. There are historical and other reasons for this – but the issue that we as dance teachers often confront is the virtual or even total illiteracy, in dance notation terms, of our students when they come to us. For that matter, there may quite possibly be some degree of insecurity on our own part. Even those students who have a grounding in dance notation are likely to have come to that only through their A-level studies – which is probably very late on in their dancing experience.

Thus we have a situation in which competent dancers are asked to learn dance notation from scratch. The difficulty lies in relating the basics of movement notation to sometimes quite sophisticated – and always quite ambitious – ideas about what dance can be. (I remember this myself, only too well – 'How am I going to get to what I want to do from something as basic and boring as *step gesture step gesture*?') Perfectly understandable – and despite our best efforts, most students – and even dance programmes! – choose to drop notation studies when they can.

But perhaps the leap from one to the other is not as far as you might think; and in this book we hope to show this.

The book falls into two main parts, as follows:

Part 1

- Six short choreographic studies, notated in two levels of difficulty.
- Ideas for working with the studies choreographically, performatively and analytically.
- A commissioned music score designed to accompany each study (score and CD).
- Notes on the structure and style of each study in general, and relating to the work of the specific choreographer on whose output it is based.
- Pointers to other choreographers for the reader to explore by way of comparison.
- A list of references to aid further research into these choreographers.
- A list of alternative music suggestions to experiment with.
- A glossary of notation symbols and terms (with each study) to aid the novice reader (and teacher).

Part 2

- o Scholarly essays on:
- o Philosophical issues in choreographic style
- o Philosophical perspectives on performance style
- o Performance, choreography and documentation.
- o An annotated bibliography, focusing on useful notation texts in particular.

Notation is the unifying factor, because without notation other aspects of dance study are very difficult, and even impossible on certain levels. The themes that are explored through creative engagement with notation are continued and developed through the essays in Part 2.

- — Documentation. Notation is a means of documentation. It is far more detailed and precise than video, far less ambiguous and tortuous than verbal description, and a great deal more reliable than memory (which is the traditional method, of course, and certainly not one to be ignored – see the essays by Sarah Whatley and Rachel Duerden in Part 2).
- — Analysis/research. If you can read notation, you have access to the hundreds of dances that have been notated – both for reconstruction purposes and for analytical study. (Musicians and actors take this for granted.) Through the score, we can gain insights into the work, make comparisons, trace developments, identify innovations and so on (see Bonnie Rowell's essay in Part 2).
- — Choreography. Access to other choreographers' work through notation offers a great deal to developing choreographers, who can learn from those who have gone before them. A notated score allows for detailed and leisurely scrutiny of the inner workings of a dance, its structure at every level, movement vocabulary and leitmotifs, themes, cross-connections, relationship with its music, and so on. It offers a wonderful resource of choreographic ideas with which the developing choreographer can engage and experiment.
- — Performance. The same applies if we approach the dance-work as performers – the score shows exactly the anatomical movement intended by the choreographer, rather than *one* dancer's interpretation of it that we may see on film, for example. It shows the 'how' of movement, not simply the 'what'. Through this kind of detail, students can teach themselves about technique, performance and interpretation (see Sarah Whatley's essay).

With these things in mind, we have created a collection of half a dozen short notated dance studies, presented in Part 1. Prefacing the studies are detailed explanations of ways to use them:

- —As practice material in reading notation
- —As choreographic themes or strings of themes to be explored in workshops
- —As scores to be analysed for their structure and choreographic detail
- —As reference points for discussion and explanation of choreographic style in relation to professional choreographers.

The different levels of complexity in the studies, which are rendered in **elementary** and in more **advanced-level notation**, allow not only for testing reading skills to a higher level, but also for examining choreographic possibilities. In other words, each individual study shows both an example of a relatively simple choreographic structure and *one* way of giving it lots of stylistic detail. It could itself be varied, developed, given further detail by the student, and/or discussed in relation to other choreographers' work.

Each study has begun from **a particular choreographer** – so each is, in its most complex manifestation, a kind of choreographic style study (a short dance 'in the style of' Jonathan Burrows, Lucinda Childs or whomever).

In the **simplified version** of each, various details have been taken out, thus opening up the possibilities for students to engage with it in different ways and with different choreographers in mind. So the first version of the dance that we see is like a **sketch**. We can manipulate it, colour it, inflect it as we will, as a choreographer or as a performer, as a way of investigating different stylistic possibilities and relating these to professional choreographers, and so on.

The **full version** of the score offers *one way* of developing that original material, one that captures something of **an individual choreographer's approach**.

By engaging with the material in these different ways, drawing on the range of skills the dancers are developing – in performance, choreography, critical analysis and understanding of different choreographers' work – they will, we hope, gain a better sense of the **inter-relatedness** of all those strands, as well as a more confident grasp of notation itself and recognition of its potential. In Figure 1 below a still figure is notated in two different ways. Each version implies something slightly different about the intended performance and choreographic style. (See p. 15.)

The three scholarly essays in Part 2 focus on the notions of 'choreographic style' and 'performance style', with detailed reference to professional work and to the issues surrounding the identification and analysis of 'style', and on the role and function of Labanotation, comparing it with music notation, play texts, video and other documentary forms.

There is an annotated bibliography. In addition to selected references to choreographers mentioned and to appropriate theoretical and critical writing, it contains is a broader selection of references encompassing textbooks and study guides for notation, professional scores of choreographies, articles on the teaching, development and use of Labanotation, critical-analytical articles including Labanotation as an illustrative tool, writing on dance and sport.

Figure 1

Part 1: Choreographic Studies

1.1: Using the studies

'It's not what you know, it's the way that you know it!'

The key aim here is to explore how to get to an idea of 'style' – both choreographic style and performance style – from the written text, through exploring the relationships between the dancer and the dance, and between the dance and its documentation. Practical and theoretical approaches are closely integrated throughout.

The studies in this book offer opportunities for:

1. Reading/reconstruction experience at different levels
2. Investigating choreographic style, in performance and through analysis, with reference to contemporary choreographers
3. Choreography workshops/movement studies
4. Developing a sketchbook of choreographic ideas
5. Being creative with a knowledge of other choreographers, or giving a stylistic inflection to a study, based on a choreographer
6. Exploring the role and function of music in choreography
   The above areas are expanded upon below, both in a general application, and in the context of individual studies.

i.
Reading and reconstruction

The scores offer reading and reconstruction experience at different levels, including consideration of the choices made in notating the study.

A score is a way of recording or documenting a dance, but at the same time it is an interpretation of an existing dance. A number of issues will crop up when considering the studies, especially the more advanced ones: why did the notator choose to notate the movement in *this* way rather than *that*? (See 'Analysing choreographic style' below.) What does that suggest about the choreographic intentions?

Another distinction may be made between notating the *general idea* of a movement or phrase, and notating it in all its detail. Bar 4 of Study 3 illustrates this.

In the simple version (**Figure 2**), the descent to the floor is indicated clearly but without explanation of how to achieve it – e.g. is the body allowed to be involved in compensatory movement? Should the arms remain exactly where they are throughout?.

In the complex version (**Figure 3**), these details are added, making it clearer how the movement should be executed, but also adding a degree of constraint by not allowing for as much individual interpretation of the choreography.

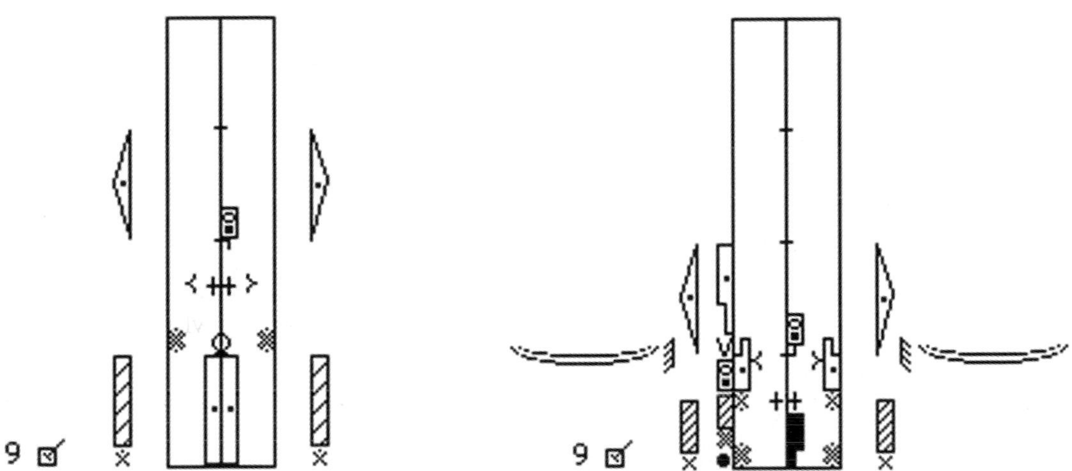

Figure 2

Figure 2 shows that the knees bend a lot, and the supports change from feet to hips and then the back – so you sink right down until you are sitting on the floor, then lie back.

Figure 3

Figure 3 shows the same, but with more description of how you get there: a step backwards, dropping the centre of weight, sliding the hands out along the floor as you roll down the spine to a lying position.

Depending on the choreographic intention, either of these approaches to notation may be appropriate. The descent to the floor could be intended to be executed as smoothly and easily as possible; if this is more important than the exact placement of the arms or body at any given moment, every dancer is likely to achieve it differently, and hence the sketchier notation is the one to use, because it contains sufficient information to convey this. However, if it is more important to the choreography to have the movement *exactly* as originally conceived, regardless of which dancer executes it, then the detailed version will be required – at least for accurate documentation purposes, and for insights into the choreographic intention. These considerations help to bring the score alive for the dancer, and thus also help in the process of reconstruction by making sense of the score *as a dance*, rather than a set of unconnected movements.

ii.
Analysing choreographic style

Applying the theories outlined above, the studies may be approached with reference to contemporary choreographers (comparing issues in the notation with 'real' choreographies).

You can do this practically through performance (performing and thus embodying an understanding of the style) or as an academic research exercise (scrutinising the score, identifying distinctive features).

For analysis purposes, each is a score in miniature, offering insights into a choreographer's style, identifying features that recur or stand out in some way, identifying the range of movement choices and structural decisions and so on.

For example, a simple position may be notated in different ways according to the notator's interpretation of attributes such as the intended dynamic, movement qualities and attack (see 'Reading and reconstruction' above).

Figure 4: the separate descriptions for different parts of limbs tells you what the SPATIAL DESIGN of the image is. (The limb pre-signs indicate which part of arm or leg goes where in space, suggesting a potentially sculptural effect.)

Figure 5: the use of contraction theory here gives a DYNAMIC dimension, drawing attention to the muscular effort involved in moving into the image. (The general direction for each arm and leg is shown, and the contraction pre-signs indicate the degree to which the extremity is brought closer to the point of attachment. Note that here the rotation symbol for the leg is necessary to achieve the exact shape.)

Figure 4 emphasises sculptural shape in space (by giving individual symbols to each part of each limb, highlighting their equal importance); while **Figure** 5 emphasises the tension and effort in making the movement (through the use of contracted gestures, the sense of contraction implying a degree of tension).

You can imagine the same image or snapshot appearing in a Martha Graham choreography, such as *Cave of the Heart* (1946) or *Errand into the Maze* (1947), and equally in a work by Merce Cunningham. The notation, however, gives the reader an insight into the performance of the movement, in terms of the choreographer's likely intentions. (Which version would you associate with either of these choreographers?)

In Study 2, bar 2, beat 3, the arm gestures (**Figure 6**) could equally well be notated using contracted-gesture theory in notation, emphasising the flexing of the arms to take the hands towards the shoulders, rather than the shape described in space by the placement of lower and upper arms individually (**Figure 7**).

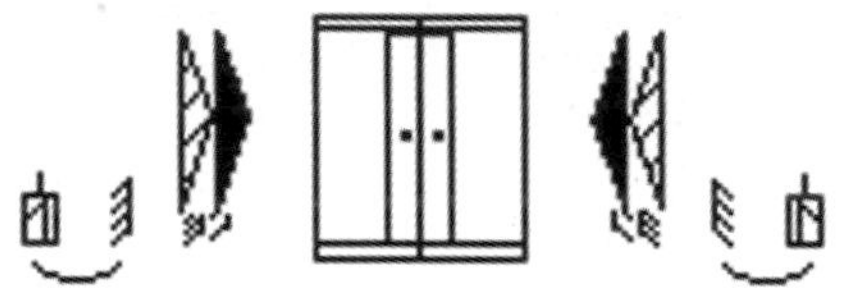

Figure 6

Here each part of the arm is given its own direction and level, as if the upper and lower arms have an independent existence.

Figure 7

Here, the arms are notated side middle, but with four degrees of contraction, bringing the hand much closer in towards the point of attachment (shoulder) – but only enough to bring it to the opposite shoulder and not to its own.

When notating this particular study, I chose the method shown in **Figure 6**, because the choreographer's intention appeared to me to suggest a pedestrian, non-dramatic quality, creating a shape in space. If there had been a sense of the arms closing in on the body – like a shiver or a hug – then contraction theory would probably have been more appropriate.

A good exercise would be to try these out in the studio, to get the different feel of each: approaching the position either as a shape to be copied, like a statue or a picture, or as a state of dynamic tension, a moment of change, being poised for action. (See also Bonnie Rowell's essay in Part 2.) The point here is that there are insights to be gleaned about choreographic style, which may be understood through academic analysis or in an embodied way through performance, both with reference to the score.

iii.
Choreography workshops

Each study can be many different dances.

For example, you can treat the whole score or a section or motif as a theme to be developed and varied in the creation of an entirely new dance.

You can follow a single strand (such as supports only, or arm gestures only) through the study, as in **Figure 8**.

You might unpack an individual 'moment' (**Figure 9**), which may offer a starting point for a choreographic exploration.

In these ways, notation is drawn upon as an analytical tool to be used when devising workshops in choreography.

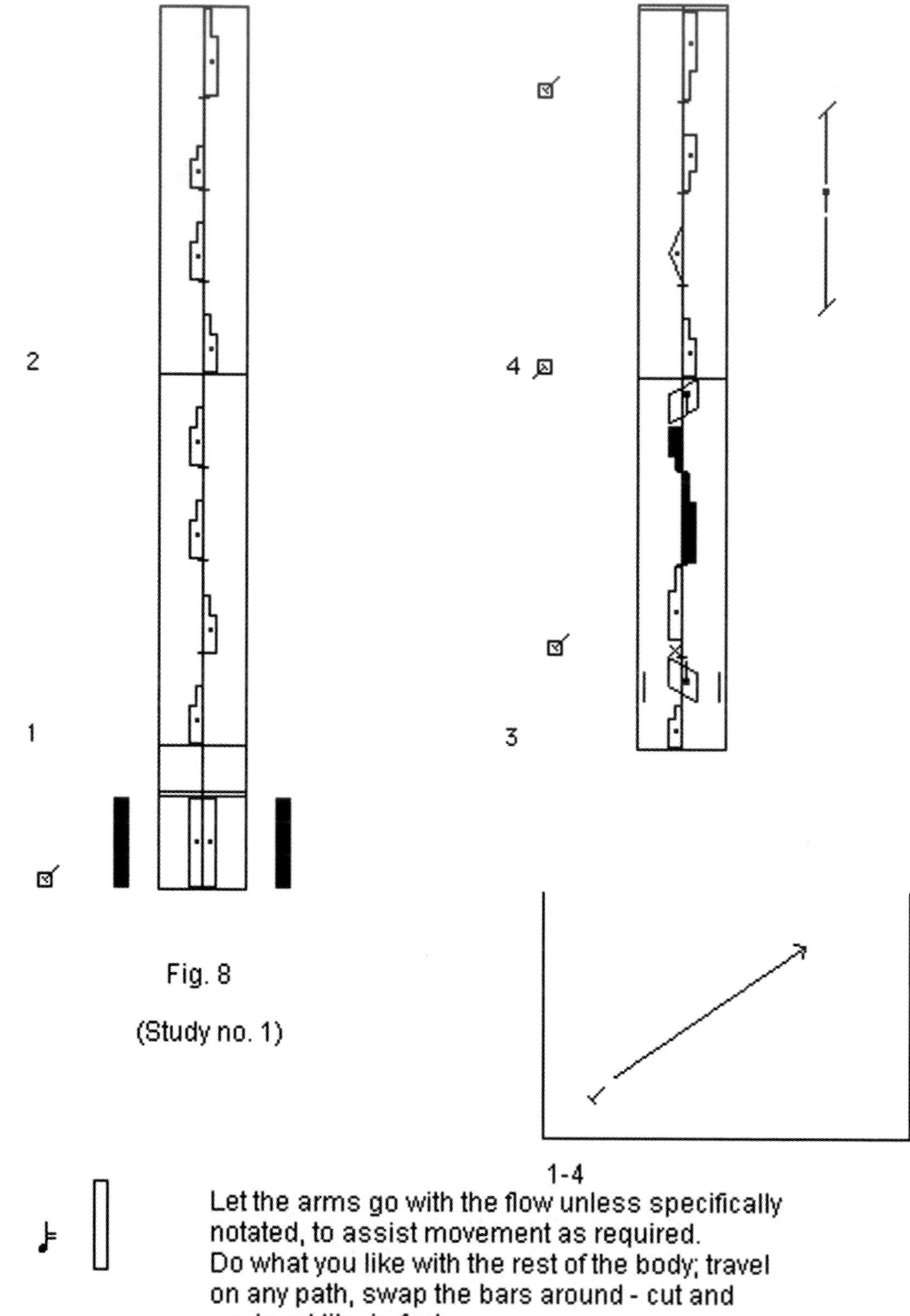

Fig. 8

(Study no. 1)

Let the arms go with the flow unless specifically notated, to assist movement as required.
Do what you like with the rest of the body; travel on any path, swap the bars around - cut and paste ad lib., in fact.

Fig. 9

(Study no. 2)

Here, the upper arm is side low, and lower arm side high, hands touching front of shoulder. The head turns and rotates to the right, allowing the shoulder section to be included in the movement a little (in notation terminology, an 'inclusion bow' shown by the bracket), and the focus is diagonally forwards low.
This moment may offer an idea about an emotional state which could be the starting point for a dance.

You can use the studies as a stimulus for playing with choreographic devices and processes to assist you in your ability to create dances and dance material.

Using the notation scores, you can use a 'pick and mix' or 'cut and paste' approach to putting movement, moments or phrases together. This will provide an array of compositional potential, involving stylistic and logistical choices, which will, we hope, lead you to create your own intricate material and dances.

Some suggestions are simple, others more complex, but they should all help with your practical experience in dance making. Once you have learnt a study, doing sequences or whole studies in reverse, retrograde or laterally transferring the material (from one side of the body to the other) will easily provide a range of ideas and potential for making your own dances. Although the studies attempt to look at stylistic aspects of dance movement, they were nearly all created by the same team, so you may find some inherent stylistic similarities – something to look out for, perhaps. The ideas suggested in this section may apply to any of the studies in the book; you can use the studies as a scrapbook for making a collage of movement.

In short, you can apply all the familiar choreographic devices to any part or the whole of any study! Below are some examples of ways of working with the material.

Example 1:

Select or create very short phrases (movements), only from half a bar up to two bars long. Generate some that travel and have a sense of direction, while others can be relatively still, in-place or even slow moving.

This can be done by an individual or as a small group, where you could learn each other's phrases and not have to create too many yourself. Number or letter each of your phrases, and cut and paste the labels in any order. How many variations are possible? (Think 'the National Lottery'. If you have 49 phrases – that's only 25 people in a class creating two phrases each, and with one to spare – and you start sequencing them logically, around fourteen million combinations are available to you from using just six short 'moments'!)

By selecting and sequencing your moments into a longer phrase, you will probably have a dance that incorporates a wide range of dynamics for you to explore either as a starting point for a whole dance or to provide a wide range of variation to the dance as it exists.

The studies can be starting points for a longer dance. Each one has something that should interest or stimulate you in some way.

Example 2:

Study 5 is a study for the arms only. This allows for a great deal of potential for what to do with the rest of your body and where you are in the space: on the floor, sitting in a chair even. Again, the way you perform it, the speed and the dynamic can offer a full range of choreographic options. The studies are written in bars with a set timing; this is to help you read and understand them in relation to the main purpose of this book, but you are free to lengthen or shorten the movements to suit your own ideas.

You could travel this study around the room – it has the potential to become something very loosely regimented, slow, processional: somewhat in the style of a Pina Bausch promenade phrase, as seen in her piece *1980*. Or it could be merged with a running-type phrase, such as **Study 1**, offering a completely different experience. Alternatively, you could play with the material in a spatial way by utilising Trisha Brown's clever CUBE task.[1] Having learnt the arm phrase, you can be directed to a completely different space around you by using this apparently restrictive, though eventually liberating, choreographic device. The device will guide you to numerous points around the body through the concept of a numbered grid pattern in the shape of a cube, and an arbitrary letter/number code provides the sequencing for you to make movement. Superimposing one set of structures over another will provide a gratifying amount of movement material to explore and cultivate.

Study 5b shows one simple way of developing the study, by incorporating steps and movements of the torso.

What follow are some further specific ideas for you to try.

[1] See the chapter on Brown in Livet, A. (1978) *Contemporary Dance,* New York, Abbeville Press.

Spatial design (1)

Study 1, for example, is based on step patterns incorporating two main aspects: **footwork** and the **direction** of the movement (floor pattern). One simple thing to do first is to notice how the floor patterns work. Draw the three floor patterns (**Figure 10**) from this study on top of each other in one floor-plan box. What shape do you get? Where does it start and end and where do you go to whilst tracing it? You can now carry out simple tasks to explore the potential of floor patterns.

Walk the shape. Try walking the shape: forwards, backwards, sideways, adding simple turns, changing your focus/front, adding in a few small leaps or hops.

Draw your own simple floor pattern. Walk your pattern in different ways, as above. Add in jumps, hops and turns. See how comfortably fast you can perform your sequence. Keep the arms as neutral as possible, using them to help you do the footwork rather than adding complex information to the sequence. Discover what types of stepping movement suit the curves or the straight lines in your floor pattern.

Next, look at the notation in the study. You will discover that the sequence is made of simple stepping and hopping. The resulting floor pattern builds through small changes, adding a turn, changing direction, and repeating one-and-a-half bars starting with a different leg. The sense of this phrase is 'square' and sits comfortably with the beat, although we have put a tiny cross-phrase moment in towards the end of the sequence. However, there seems to be a natural logic to the way the phrase takes you from one point, through and on to the next. There is a fast, easy, effortless dynamic to the stepping and the body is held quite naturally, perhaps leaning occasionally to make a turn or a change of direction easier. You get the sense of a body moving through space, not necessarily of a character.

Try to incorporate this feel into your performance of the phrase. Once you have mastered the phrase, or you have made and mastered your own phrase, there are many simple things you can do to create some quite complex and intriguing variations for a soloist or any number of dancers.

— **Mirror the phrase:** start on the opposite side of the room and use the other foot. The phrase will return to its starting point.
— **Perform it as a duet**: dance it either mirrored or with one dancer going backwards.
— **Perform it as a quartet**: start with a dancer in each corner.
— **In canon:** try different numbers of counts between each dancer starting, perhaps even going across the phrasing in your music.
— **Perform the phrase backwards:** the turns would also go the opposite way. You might wish to work this out with a partner to help you discover which way you'll need to turn.
— **Utilise the mistakes** (from doing any of the above): choreography can be seen as a series of small experiments, which reveal a wealth of material (aka variations). The tiny 'mistakes' you make in learning the notation can be added to make new moments or developments in the dance.

Spatial Design 1: floor plans

3

2

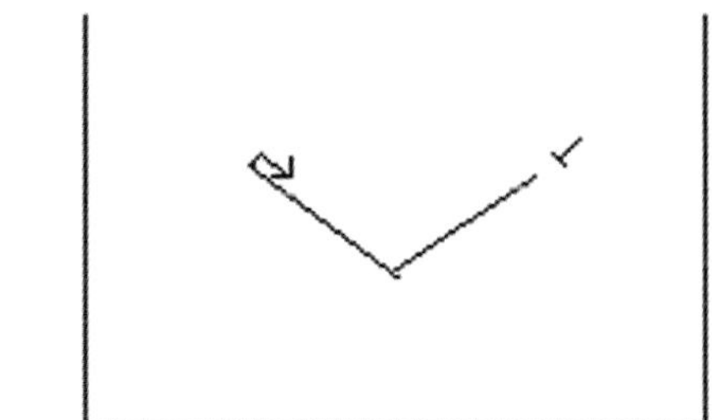

1

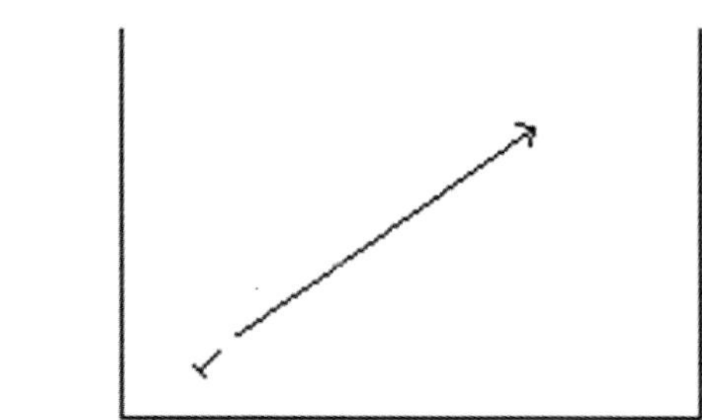

Fig. 10

These are the floor plans from Study no. 1. The open side of the box is where the audience is, and the 'pin' is the dancer. These are all drawn from the dancer's perspective.

Spatial design (2)

Keeping with the notion of floor patterns and spatial design, we find in **Study 2** that this floor pattern is less formal-looking (Figure 11). Although the study uses a pedestrian quality of movement, the pathway of the movement is interrupted, with more abrupt changes of direction than exist in **Study 1**.

You could again work on your own pathway with abrupt changes or use a colleague to create one for you (draw a little doodle and see what that creates for you spatially). What sort of movement material begins to fashion in your mind as you do this simple task? Create your own material that fits with the floor pattern you have made. Overlay patterns from members in your group and perform them simultaneously. Where there are moments of collision, make contact – create a moment of stillness or add a new contrasting or complementary quality in the movement material.

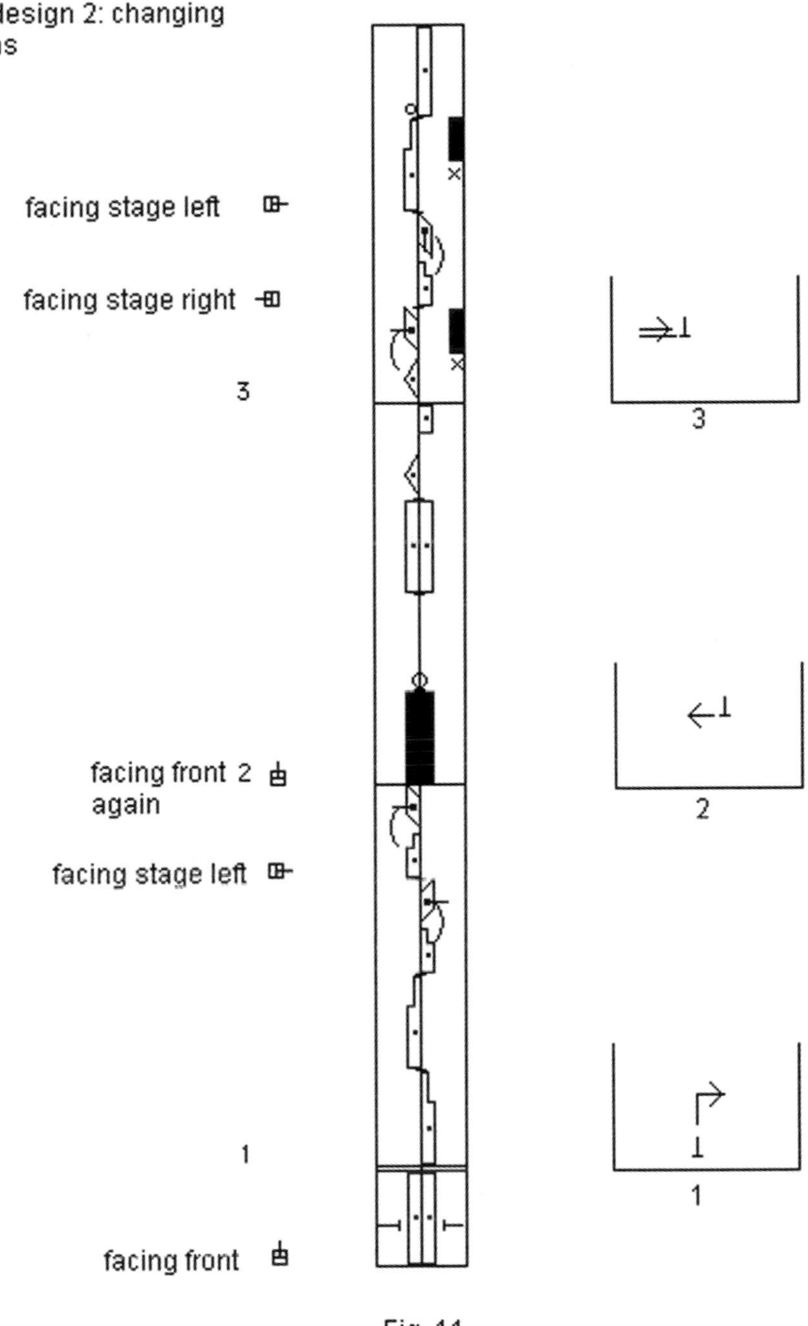

Fig. 11

The 'facing pins' in boxes show where the dancer is facing in the stage space, the point of the pin pointing in the facing direction.

Gesture

Most of the suggestions so far deal with movement ideas toward the more abstract end of a continuum. However, even when working from a pure movement stimulus, you can sometimes develop some very moving and expressive dances, because movement can and does connote specific feelings both in the performer whilst executing the movement and in audience members watching the dance.

Dance movements are often augmented with gestures or gestural movements, either complex or simple, which add depth to the meaning of the dance. Gesture plays a major role in dance making – think of Lea Anderson's work – and there is no shortage of images to help you find many varied gestures from things you see around you. Pictures in magazines can help here, or just watching people in and around town, a café or your college canteen.

Reconstruct the simple notation in Figure 12. What does this gestured movement suggest to you as you perform it or while you watch someone else perform it?.

We recognise a grand gesture for what it is: a ballet dancer in arabesque, hands clasped in prayer, a Graham contraction or a Cunningham tilt. Think of the action of an athlete winning a race, or a footballer scoring a goal: a long run with a fisted hand thrust in the air, for example.[2] Sometimes a gesture is iconic or symbolic (maybe religious, as suggested), while at other times it is, perhaps, more emotive – sorrowful, or, as in the sporting example, elated and joyful. Gestures can come out of the physical energy involved in doing a movement. Discover and play with strength and energy in a movement to create the gesture. For example, look at bars 7 and 8 in **Study** 4 (notice the 'effort' symbol, showing dynamic quality).

Both Graham and Cunningham use grand (full-body) gestures. These may be abstract, defining the body in space (Cunningham), or more immediately connected to specific feelings or emotional experiences (Graham). The same gesture can suggest a different feeling or tone depending on the energy and dynamic you use to execute the movement. Here we can refer back to our example right at the beginning of the Introduction, where we offer you the same 'shape' but re-presented by the notation in two different ways; one offers a more dramatic impact, the other a more abstract or sculptural impression. A specific movement within a sequential dance phrase may suggest a reading or meaning in that context, but in isolation the specific movement itself may insinuate numerous suggestions to be explored.

For more ideas, try looking at paintings (such as Pablo Picasso's *Women running on the Beach,* 1922) or sculptures for inspiration. These provide a wealth of gestural material for you to explore. Look at 'old master' paintings, especially for figure and scene, or even stained-glass windows in churches to find images to use.

[2] *The Archie Gemmell Goal*: see the annotated bibliography.

Gesture

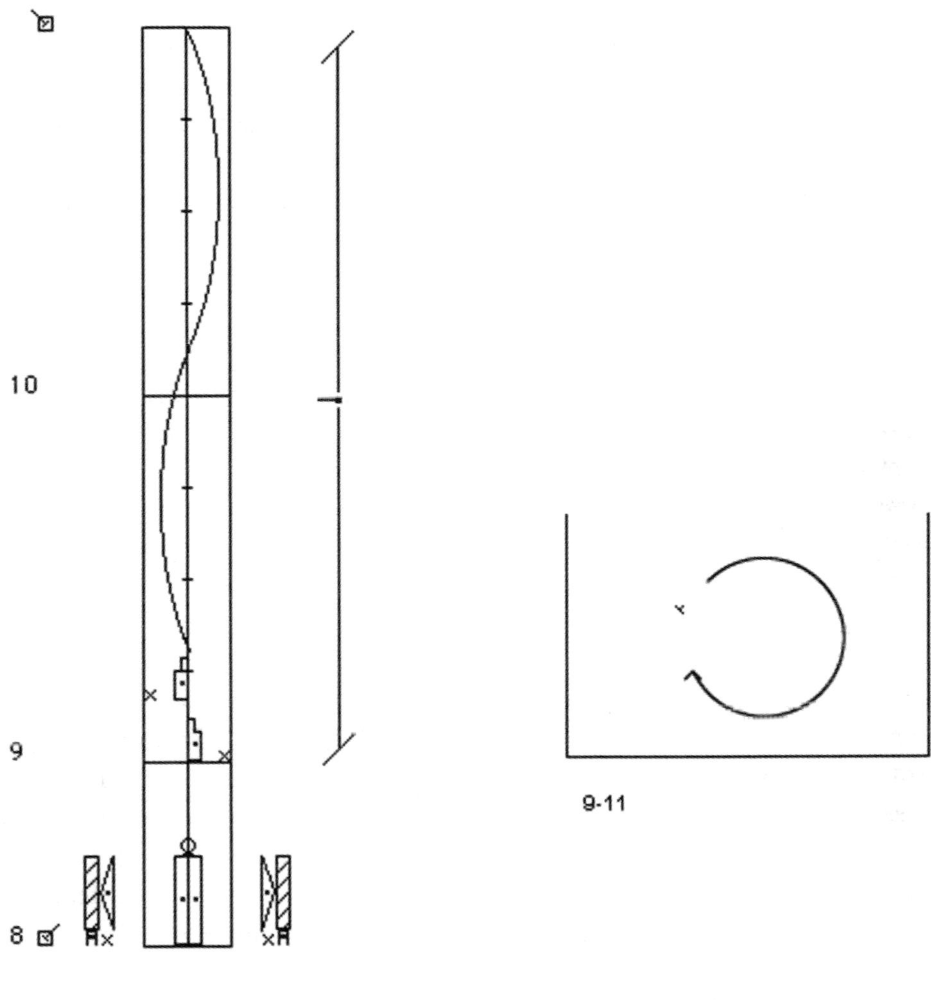

Fig. 12

This could be seen as an 'euphoric' moment - the upward-facing palms, the running steps around the performance space in a sweeping circular pathway.

Mood, character, dynamic

As discussed so far, some of the studies try to retain an identifiable dynamic range throughout, which is perhaps a conscious stylistic feature of that particular study. However, dynamic range gives colour and texture to the movement. Going back to our 'cut and paste' idea, we could explore dynamics in a playful way similar to how we explored the pathways tasks (see tasks and ideas at the beginning of this section).

A mood, emotional state or small quirk **is** embedded in each study, and these might present you with starting points for your own dances. Although the studies are quite short, a dance can be created or devised relatively easily from a single image or moment from any one of the studies. As mentioned earlier, often when you are starting out in choreographing, making the first movement or choosing your first idea can be difficult. During their dance training and education, students are sometimes taught to do well-known movements and not necessarily encouraged to be imaginative. There is a considerable amount of material within these studies to get you going.

For example, **Study 3** (Figure 13) has a defined focal point – this might be an idea to start from. The character starts and ends the short phrase having established a point in space of identifiable interest to the dancer. You could create your own dance by being inventive about who or what is in the space, what is outside the space, or what might be a distinct attraction or fascination about a particular point in space. Might it repulse you or attract you, does it move, and how might you react to it, if it did?.

These simple moments can offer a range of images and emotional states for you to explore as a theme for a whole dance. Sometimes (we speak from personal experience) trying to come up with a starting point for a dance is the most difficult part but not always the most important. Use the notation scores to make that first move and then, once you have a few movements, your imagination and critical faculties will soon come into play in making your own original dance.

By approaching these studies in an open and resourceful way, very quickly you should be able to get your own movement ideas from the studies and create new dances for yourself.

Mood, character, dynamic

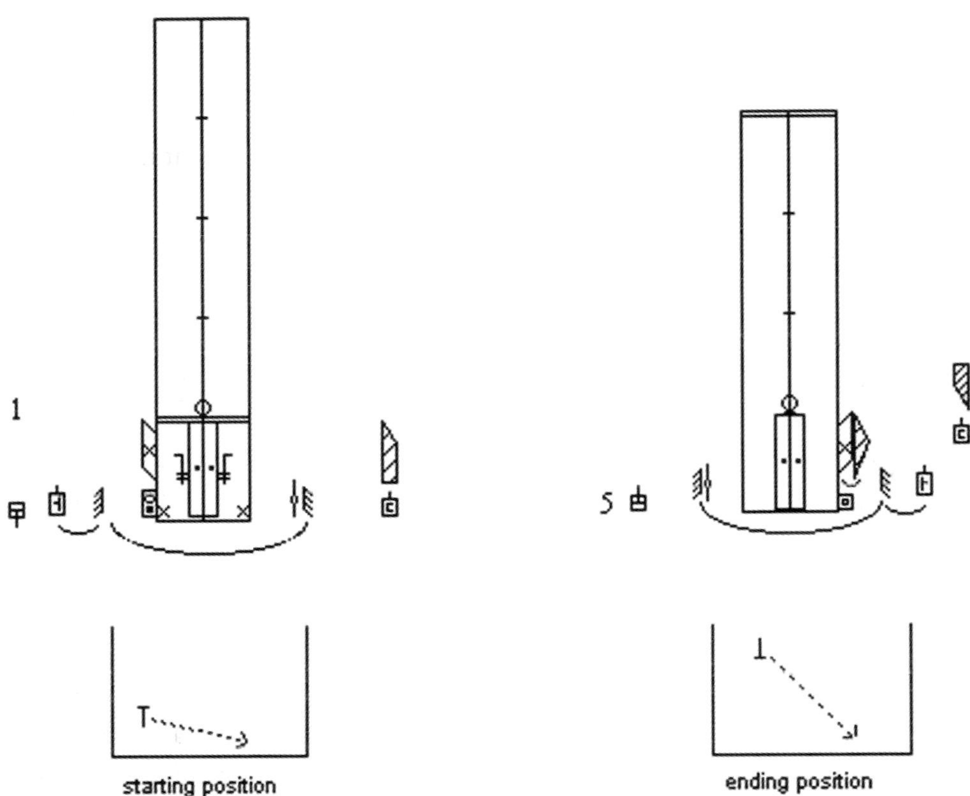

Fig. 13

In each case here the hands are placed on one hip, one on top of the other (shown by the white pin). The focus is to the same spot in space, but the dancer is facing a different direction each time, hence the slightly different position of the body.
The small floor plans are included here to illustrate the direction of 'looking', shown by the dotted line.

iv.
Choreographic sketchbook

Each study offers suggestions for how to capture movement ideas in notation.

For example, the 'simple' version of each study may be seen to contain or imply the complex version, showing how a dance may be captured in notation at an elementary level.

Conversely, the additional details in the complex version contribute to the sense of a particular style, and you can record these things in a 'choreographic notebook' by analysing the results of improvisation in workshops to identify the salient features of a phrase (for example: it turns, it includes body tilts, it travels) and record a sketch of the idea.

Choreographic ideas may be expressed in motif writing (see the final chapter of the *Elementary Study Guide to Labanotation*, or Ann Hutchinson's *Motif Description: New writing developments* (1984)) or, alternatively, a few key symbols may be used as an *aide mémoire*, capturing some significant features such as (see Figure 14):

Directions – whether of movement through space or gesture

Chest tilts

Slightly lowered centre of gravity

Travelling as much as possible

Successive movements or gestures

Body key

Floor patterns

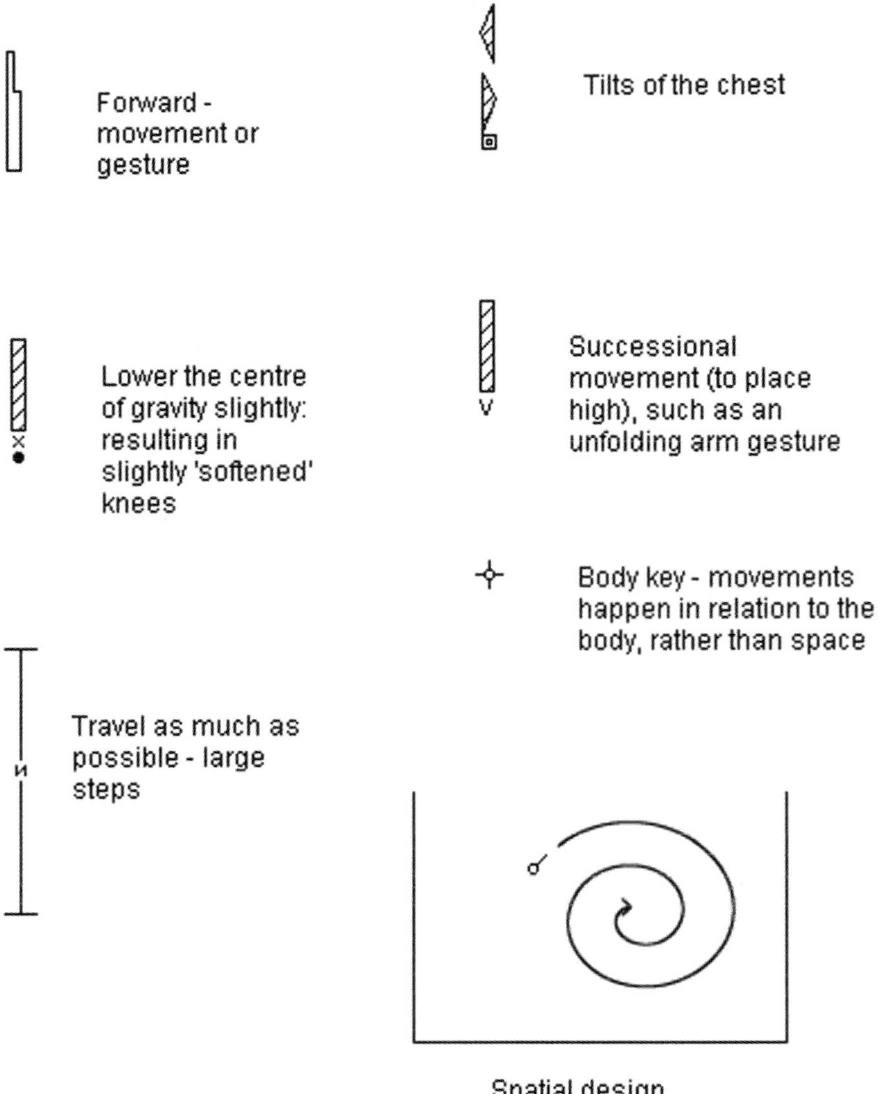

Fig. 14

A few examples of symbols that could be used to indicate general ideas or as an aide memoire to choreography.

You could start to compile your own vocabulary of notation symbols for your own use: something like *The Dancer's Glancer* (1992), for example, but containing the symbols that are important and relevant to you and your work. What is also interesting (as well as useful) about doing this is that it can show you quite quickly and visually what your choreographic preferences are.

V.
Creative engagement with notation

All the points above illustrate the potential for notation to be central to both creative and analytical work; combining these in another way is the exploration of the notion of 'choreographic style'.

The simple studies, for example, offer the opportunity to experiment with and apply your knowledge and understanding of the work of professional choreographers, adding complexity and stylistic nuance to the study by incorporating different elements of dynamic, rhythm, spatial design and other attributes. This encourages you to embody your understanding of different choreographic styles, and to use that knowledge creatively in attending to a choreographer's specific movement choices, impulses, expressive devices, structuring devices and so on.

Experiments in choreographic style study ideas (using Study 2 as an exemplar)

Using the simple version, reconstruct the first four bars. Notice what is happening in terms of steps, turns, directions and gestures. Notice the spatial design, and the timing of the phrase overall. When the phrase is fully embodied – that is, you can perform it from memory, giving attention to the sense of the phrase as a whole rather than individual movements – then begin to experiment with it, giving it different stylistic inflections based on your knowledge of dance styles and choreographic styles. For instance:

— Cunningham – perhaps add tilts, extensions, isolations.
— Ballet – add turn-out, rounded arms; perhaps steps become *chassés* or *posés*.
— Siobhan Davies – perhaps drop the centre of gravity a little, allow the movement to develop a weighty swing, or involve arms and body more.

Below are three slightly modified versions of the four-bar phrase.

— The first (Figure 15) is based on ideas from Cunningham's work – including tilts and rotations of the upper torso, extensions, and the use of turn-out on the *retiré*.
— The second (Figure 16) introduces very little change in terms of steps and gestures, simply dropping the weight and allowing a natural momentum to influence the paths of the gestures. This version was influenced by Siobhan Davies' choreography.
— The third (Figure 17) similarly introduces little change in terms of steps and gestures, but includes turn-out as a standard feature, slightly rounded arms, characteristically held just in front of the body, and a mostly upright torso.

Adding a 'Cunningham' flavour, with additional leg gestures and body tilts.
The 'body key' symbol: inside the square bracket in bar 4, indicates that the arms relate to the body, rather than space i.e. the arms here 'feel' side middle and then place high, although to the observer they are creating diagonal lines in relation to up and down.

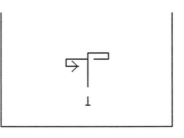

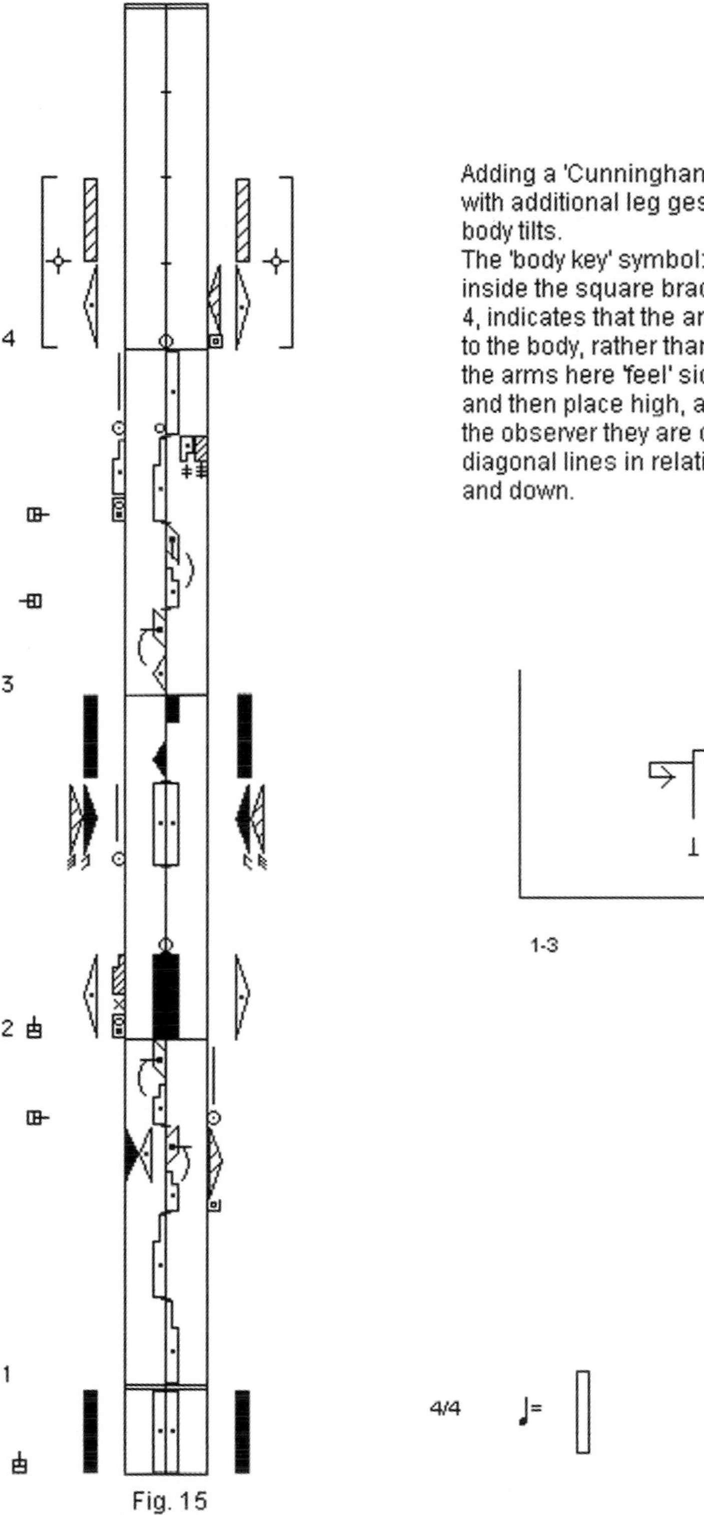

Fig. 15

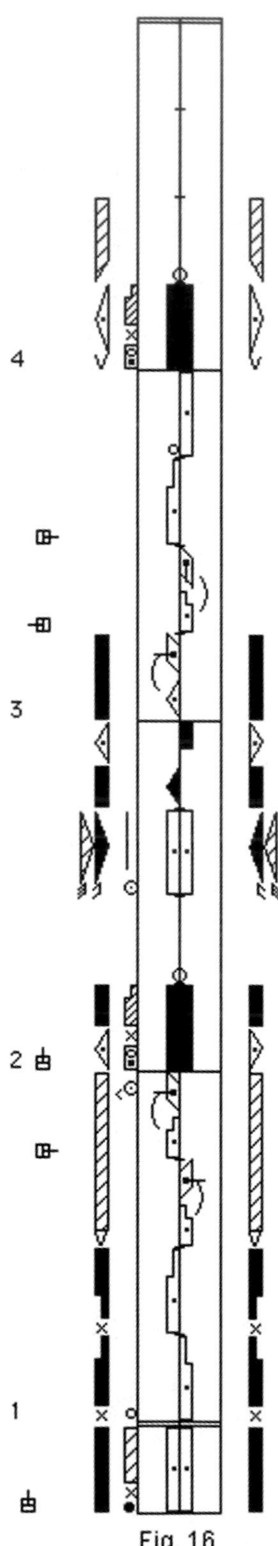

Fig. 16

Adding a 'Davies' flavour, with the slight dropping of the centre of weight at the beginning, which results in a heavier, more 'weighted' feel and softened knees; more arm gestures moving in arcs forwards and backwards, or sideways, with successional movements shown in bars 1 and 4:

Also some gentle contractions of the torso in a forwards high tilt:

The final position suggests bird imagery, perhaps.

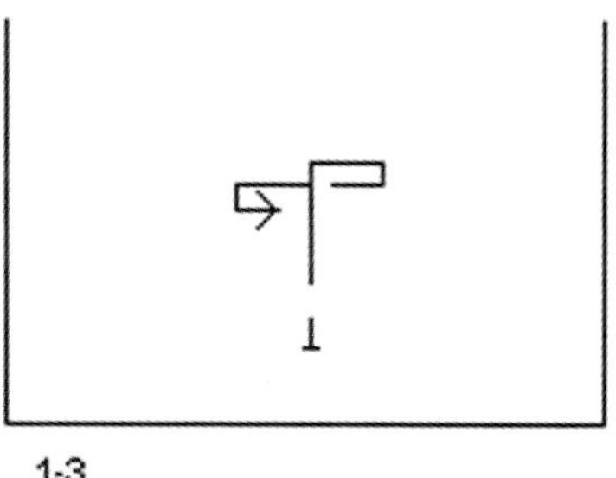

1-3

4/4 ♩=

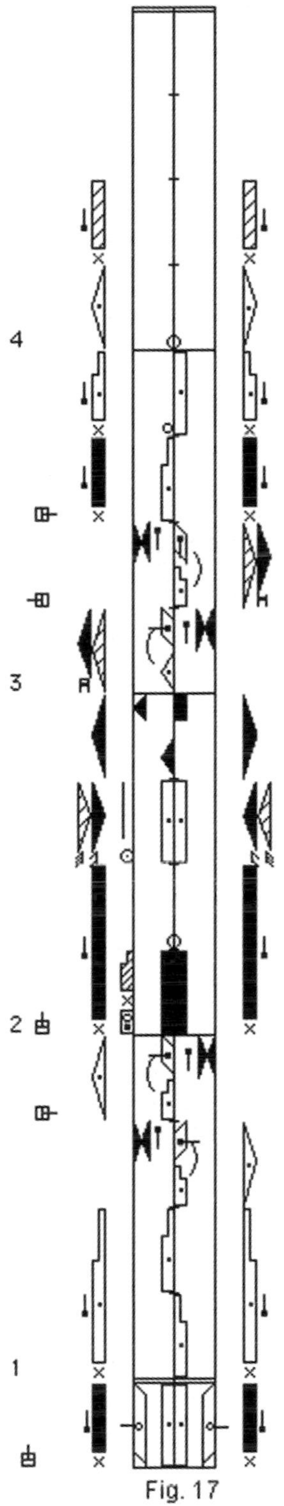

Fig. 17

Adding a 'ballet' flavour through the introduction of turn-out (rotation symbols in the leg gesture columns at the start), rounded arms (one-degree of contraction), and upright torso for the most part.

The black pins by the arm gesture symbols indicate that the position is slightly in front of the body.

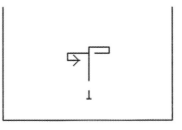

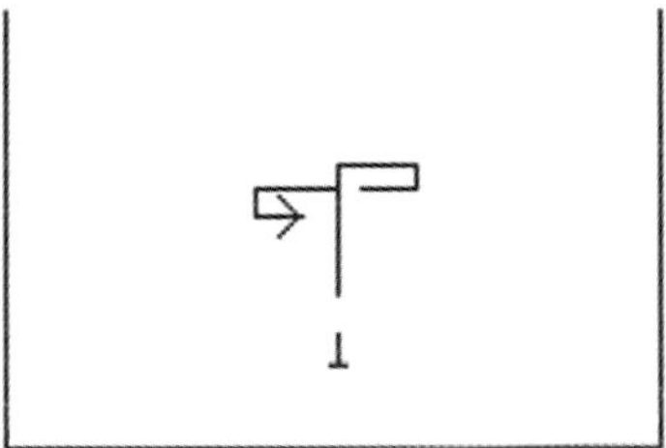

1-3

4/4 ♩=

Looking at the three side by side encourages critical reflection on the range of possibilities open to the choreographer, and the very different effects achieved through different stylistic inflections – through analysing exactly what the differences are, and how they work.

The notation of the 'Cunningham' study shows an emphasis on sculptural shapes, tilts and twists of the torso. It is possible to see something of the idea of isolating parts of the body – for example, when arm or leg gestures are notated with separate directions and levels for different parts of the limbs. Notating in this way emphasises the sense of equality between and independence of different parts of the body, in comparison with, for example, a notation based on contraction of the limbs, which tends to imply movement of the limb as a whole (as noted above in relation to Martha Graham's work).

The 'softened' arms in the second version illustrate exactly this – the arm is considered as a whole, but is not pushed straight; rather, it is allowed to relax, or unfold in a successional movement. The slightly lowered centre of gravity or weight gives a weighted feel to the movement; the knees soften slightly, and the quality becomes generally more fluid.

The turn-out in the third version gives a different body-orientation straight away, as do the carefully placed arms and specific leg gestures. There is a feeling of precision similar to that of the Cunningham phrase but with a different sense of the body, which is conceived clearly as a whole-body image rather than disparate parts.

Performing the different versions helps to develop an embodied understanding of these issues: for example, through experiencing the different relationship with gravity in each of the versions, the different sense of whole-body image, and the different approaches to moving through space. (See also the *aide-mémoire* symbols in Figure 14.).

The experiment could extend from the four-bar phrase to a longer study, working with the given material and introducing other ideas. In each case, it is useful to look at and identify what is happening, what makes one different from another – for example:

- The way of holding the body
- The centre of gravity
- Timing
- Use of breath
- Musicality
- The relationship of gestures to steps
- Use of arms, legs, hands, feet, head, body, focus, etc.

All these aspects feed directly into an appreciation and understanding of other choreographers' work by developing analytical skills grounded in the real experience of movement, and applying them.

vi.
The role of music

The music we have included with the studies in this book has been composed to fit structurally with them, and we gave some indication of possible mood and dynamic to the composer as well. He has responded with some interesting and perhaps challenging scores and, for most of them, more music than you need for a single performance. You have the option, therefore, of beginning with the music and developing your own material to follow on, or of introducing your own material at the beginning and moving into the notated score – or, of course, any variation you like.

The list of alternative suggestions simply offers a range of choices to experiment with in order to see and to experience some of the different effects achieved. For example, when you are performing, how does the music affect your performance? Do you find yourself wanting to phrase the dance in a certain way, or give it a particular dynamic colouring? When you are choreographing, what effect does the music/sound/silence have on your choreography, or on your ideas for developing it? How can it stimulate without swamping?

All the material in this book is available to try with different music choices, in an experimental way (e.g. using random selection) or in relation to a particular choreographic idea of your own, or when exploring another choreographer's music choices. Below are some reminders of ways in which choreography and music may relate and choreographers and composers may collaborate:

Ways in which choreography and music can relate:

- Rhythmic and/or metric correspondence – see Lucinda Childs
- 'Peaceful coexistence' or independence – see Merce Cunningham
- Structural relationships in phrasing and instrumentation – see Mark Morris
- Radical and/or humorous juxtaposition – see Jonathan Burrows
- Economy and clarity, neither overwhelming the other – see Jennifer Jackson.

Collaborations between choreographer and composer:

- Working independently, perhaps from an agreed idea – see Cunningham and Cage
- Working closely, discussing ideas and adapting to each other's – see Siobhan Davies and various composers; Balanchine and Stravinsky
- Choreographer (or composer) making most of the decisions, giving ideas, even instructions to the other – see Shobana Jeyasingh and various composers; or, further back in time, Petipa and Tchaikovsky.

Collaborative improvisation within established structures:

- Jazz

— Siobhan Davies' *Birdsong* (2004).

These are just a few examples of different possibilities that you might like to research.

Here are some examples of writing about dance and music:

Alm, I.M. (1989), 'Stravinsky, Balanchine and Agon: An analysis based on the collaborative process', *The Journal of Musicology*, 7/2 (Spring), pp. 254–269.

Best, C. (1999), 'Why do choreographers and composers collaborate?', *Dance Theatre Journal*, 15/1, pp. 28–31.

Chamberlain Duerden, R. (1999), 'The semiotics of music and their application to dance analysis', in *Body/Language*, March, pp. 34–51.

Cunningham, M. with F. Starr (ed.) (1969), *Changes: Notes on choreography*, New York, Something Else Press.

Flood, P. (1997), 'In the silence and stillness', *Dance Theatre Journal*, 13/4, pp. 36–39.

Heaton, R. (1995), 'Music for dance', *Dance Theatre Journal*, 11/4, pp. 12–15.

Hodgins, P. (1992), *Relationships Between Choreography and Score in Twentieth-century Dance: Music, movement and metaphor*, Laviston, Queenston, Lampeter, Edwin Mellen Press.

Jordan, S. (2000), *Moving Music: Dialogues with music in twentieth-century ballet*, London, Dance Books.

Jordan, S. (1996), 'Musical/choreographic discourse: Method, music theory and meaning', in G. Morris (ed.), *Moving Words*, London, Routledge.

Kimberley, N. (1997), 'Musical collaborations', *Dance Now*, 6/1, pp. 32–36.

Lesschaeve, J. (1992), *The Dancer and the Dance*, New York and London, Marion Boyars Publications.

Pischl, A.J. & Cohen, S.J. (1963), *Composer/Choreographer*, Brooklyn, Dance Perspectives.

Preston, S. (1999), 'Dance, music and literature: The construction of meanings through an interplay of texts in Siobhan Davies's *Bridge the Distance*', in J. Adshead-Lansdale (ed.), *Dancing Texts: Intertextuality in Interpretation*, London, Dance Books.

Reich, S. (1973), 'Notes on dance and music', in R. Copeland & M. Cohen (eds) (1983), *What is Dance?* Oxford, OUP, pp. 336–8.

Roy, S. (1999), 'Part 3: Collaborations – Music', in S. Roy (ed.) *White Man Sleep: Creative insights*, London, Dance Books.

Volans, K. (1996), 'A dialogue between collaborators', *Dance Theatre Journal*, 12/4, pp. 14–17.

1.2: The Studies

Study 1

This study was inspired by the minimalist early work of Lucinda Childs. This is reflected in the simple vocabulary, the patterns and spatial design, and the fact that it could work well with a minimalist music score, such as one by Philip Glass, with whom Childs has collaborated (*Einstein on the Beach*, 1976). Childs herself has spoken about finding complexity and richness, not in the movement vocabulary itself, but in the structural relationship of her choreography with the music (*Making Dances: seven postmodern choreographers*, 1980) video cassette). In her more recent work she has shown a continuing interest in the capacity for minimal movement to be structured in a stream of variations: for example, her choreography for Scottish Opera's 2002 production of Gluck's *Orfeo ed Eurydice*. In this she moves the non-dancing chorus in uncomplicated but highly effective patterns, with simple but evocative individual gestures, creating an impression of complexity and depth through highly economical means.

The more complex version of this study reflects some of these aspects of her work, for example through its symmetrical pattern in space; the phrase could be repeated starting on the opposite foot (see workshop notes). The focus is on stepping patterns, with few gestures and little body movement – apart from 'natural' movement to assist the flow. Rhythmically the study is simple; only in the final bar is there any variation on the movement-per-beat pattern, and the phrase grows out of tiny motifs, with 'almost-repetition' – e.g. slightly varied versions of the stepping pattern, which may cross the beat, take a different direction or incorporate a turn. The overall sense is of forward movement and continuous flow, based on relaxed running, with little dynamic variation.

The study is focused on spatial design and rhythm and symmetry with variation in detail, although Childs's work is usually more complex choreographically, spatially and rhythmically, frequently reflecting visual design in floor patterns, for example, and developing structures through irregular phrase-lengths and the fragmentation of phrases and their distribution among dancers. This study could itself be treated like that, at both its simple and more complex levels, for example through breaking up the phrases into different lengths and incorporating different numbers of dancers on different pathways. (See Livet, A. [1978], *Contemporary Dance*, New York, Abbeville Press.)

Other choreographers to experiment with:

- Shobana Jeyasingh – the addition of hand gestures, a low centre of gravity and a sense of contact with the floor through the feet (*Romance... with Footnotes*, *Duet with Automobiles*)
- Paul Taylor – arm and leg gestures, springs and leaps, and use of the body (*Airs*, *Aureole*)
- Richard Alston – more use of the body in clear lines and angles (*Soda Lake*, *Shimmer*)
- Kim Brandstrup – characterisation, and incorporation of arms and body in broad movements (*Cinderella*).

Further information on these choreographers is included at the end of this section.

Study 1 plain: Notes

Nothing too complicated here. The small symbol at the top of the first page is simply to help the reader see how the jump ends – a preview of the next symbol on the following page. See also the facing pin.

Study 1 (Lucinda Childs): Notes

Contraction signs in leg gesture column: slightly bent legs.

Left-arm gestures bars 3–4: intermediate directions are used here, to show positions in between the standard 'low, middle, high, place'. So: beat 1: mid-way between place low and forward low (contracted, and in front of centre line of body); beat 3: a third towards side high from place high; next bar, end of beat 1: a third towards side middle from side low.

Pin inside bracket for leg gesture, bar 5: a deviation sign, indicating that the leg travels to back low via a sideways direction – so a 'swing round' of the leg.

Bars 8–9: parts of the foot – indicating a specific part of the foot making contact with the floor: in bar 8, beats 3 and 4, the right foot steps on the ball of the foot; in bar 9, beat 1, it lowers to flat as the left foot joins it. The legs straighten – shown in the extension sign in the leg gesture columns.

Study 1 plain

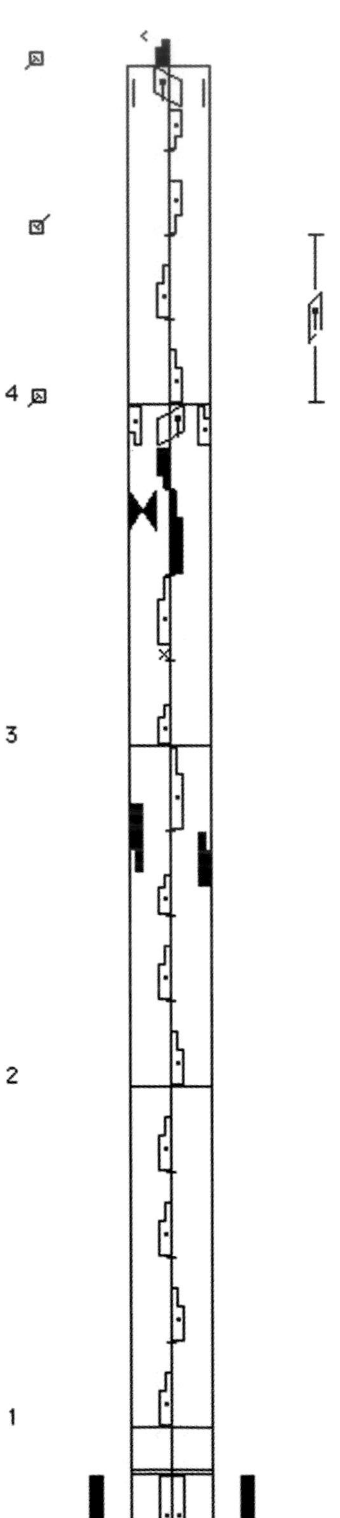

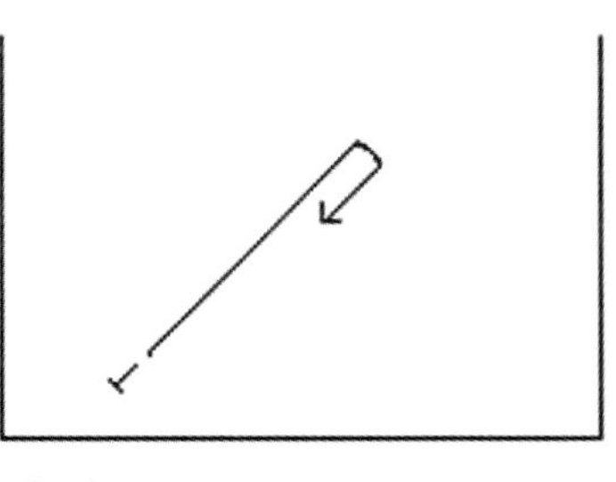

4/4 ♩ =

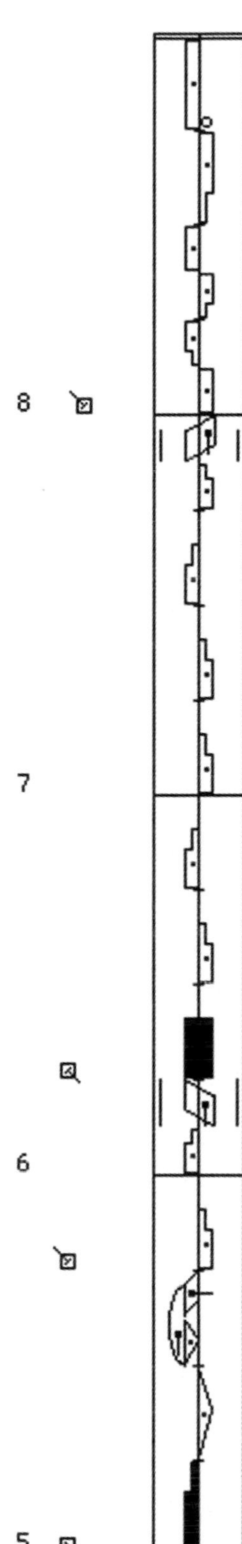

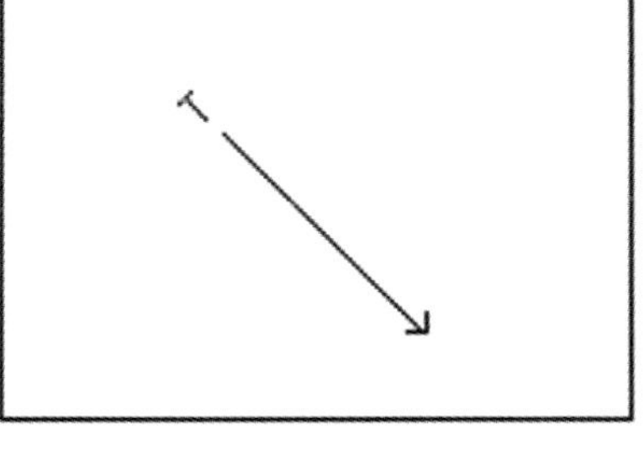

7-8

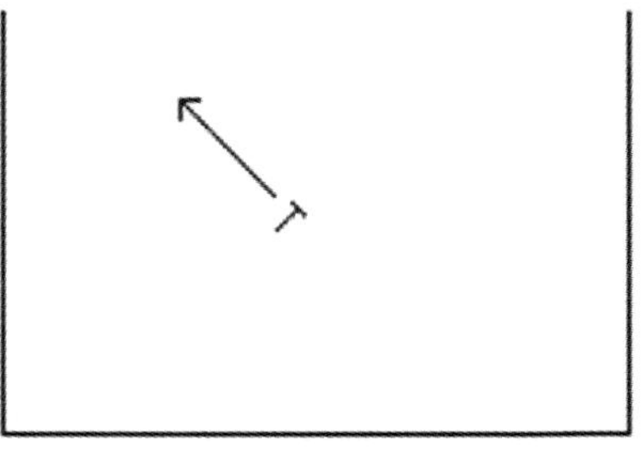

5-6

Study 1 (Lucinda Childs)

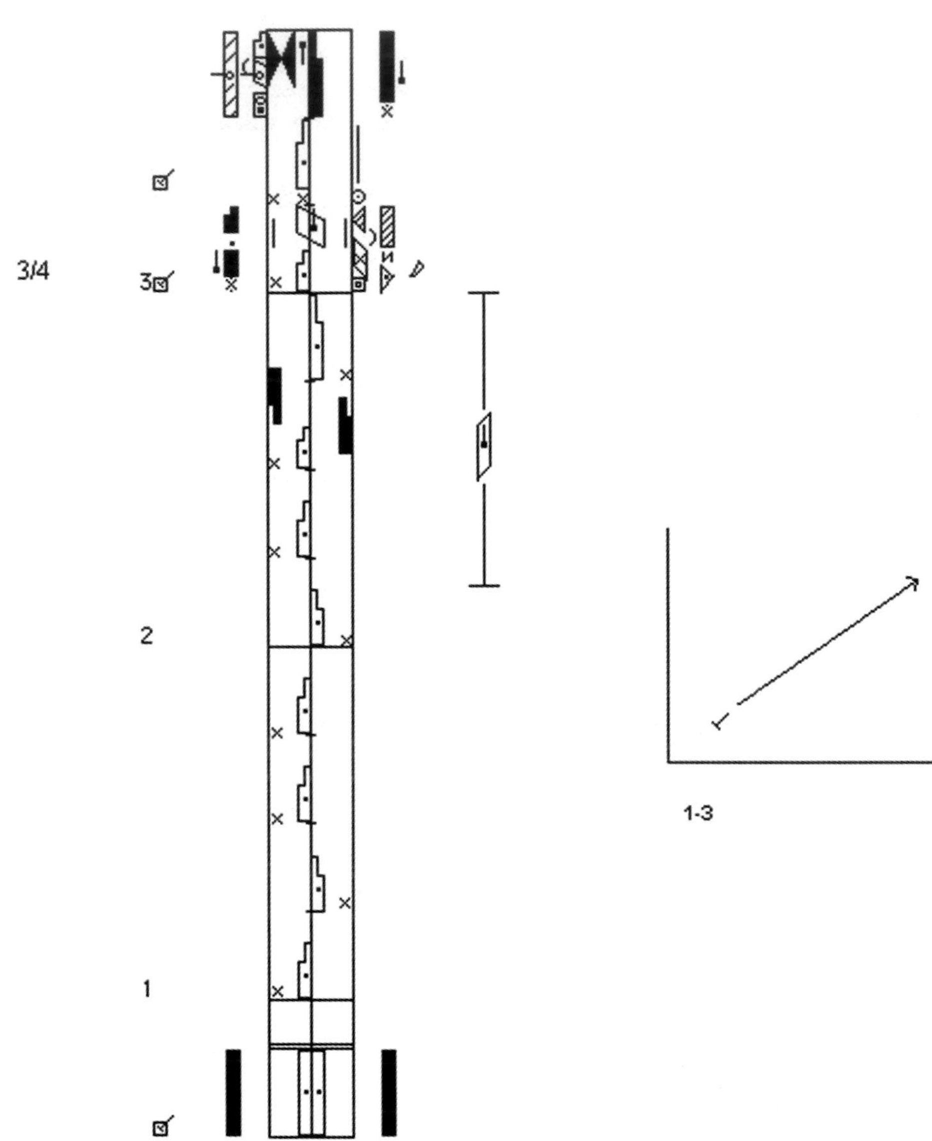

4/4 ♩ =

Let the arms go with the flow unless specifically notated, and assist movement when required.

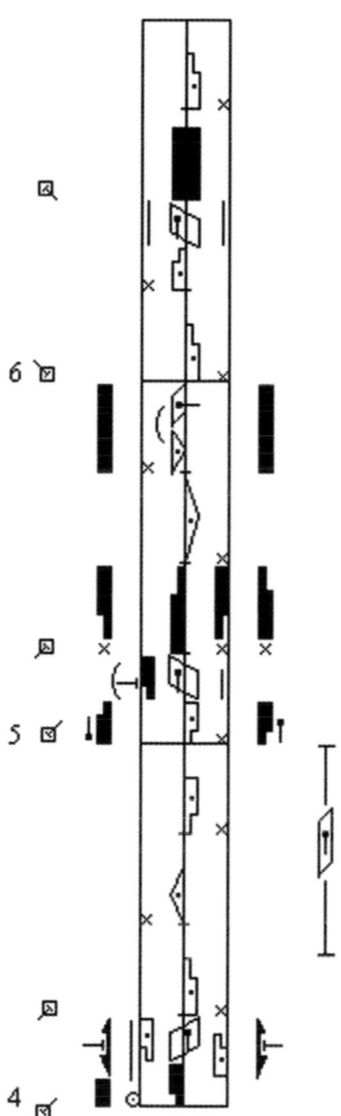

4/4

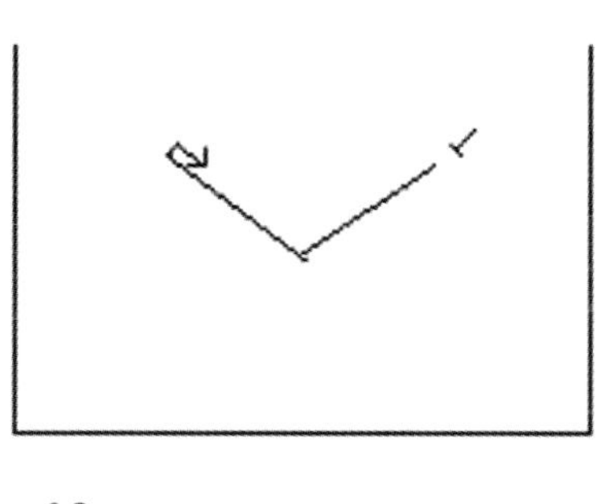

4-6

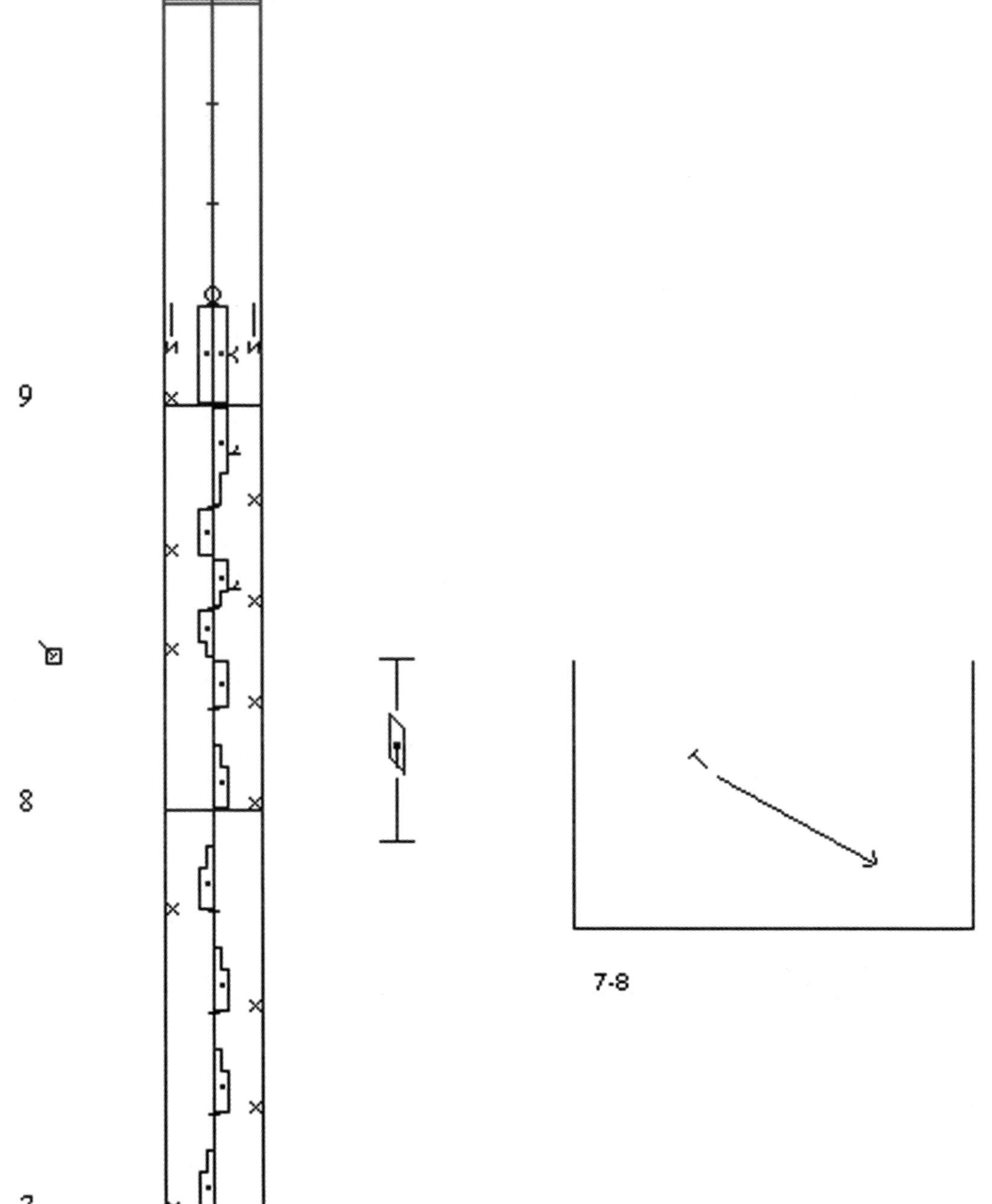
9
8
7
7-8

1

Other music suggestions

Title	Artist/composer	CD reference
Bosoe	Joe Mensah	*Rough Guide to Highlife* World Music Network RGNET 1102
Brandenburg Concerto No. 1 (1st movement)	J.S. Bach	Naxos 8.550047
Muerte de Angel	Astor Piazzolla	Naxos 8.557329
Short ride in a fast machine	John Adams	Naxos 8.559031
Do you know the way to San José?	Burt Bacharach	*The Look of Love* Warner 5046660655

Study 2

This study has taken David Gordon as its choreographic model. Like Lucinda Childs, Gordon was a member of the Judson group of experimental choreographers. His interests have been in some ways very different from hers, however. He has worked with pedestrian movement, frequently with a humorous dimension, and always with a sense of character, even when no narrative is apparent; he has said that it is important to him that his dancers 'be themselves' (see *Making Dances*).

The frequent changes of direction in this study suggest a fragmented or aimless intention, although this is to some extent counter-balanced by the apparent deliberation in the steps in bar 3, for example, where the specific gestures of the legs suggest something more precise than the 'natural' step might be. A similar effect is achieved in bar 7; the turn at the beginning of the bar gains significance coming after a moment of stillness, rather than being incorporated into a phrase. The phrases of movement have a slightly stilted quality, with sudden pauses interrupting the flow (as in the above example), creating almost a freeze-frame effect. Changes in dynamic and speed, similarly, are sudden, contributing to the disruption of flow. The movement is mostly pedestrian, but there are a few gestures that suggest significance or dramatic connotation, e.g. the 'look' in the first bar, the crossed arms in bar 2 and the 'as if hugging someone' arm gesture in bar 4, the use of fists and placement of hands.

Wearing trainers would help to get the feeling of this kind of pedestrian movement.

Other choreographers to experiment with:

— Jonathan Burrows – different music choices; use of partner work (*Stoics*, *Stop Quartet*)
— Twyla Tharp – adding jazz-influenced body movements and music (*Eight Jelly Rolls*, *Sinatra Suite*)
— Yvonne Rainer – smoothing out all dynamic inflection (*Trio A*)
— Rosemary Butcher – adding props, interacting with set or setting, involving other dancers (*Body as Site*, *Touch the Earth*)
— Anna Teresa de Keersmaeker – making it a group piece, interacting with live musicians (*Hoppla!*, *Achterland*).

Further information on these choreographers is included at the end of this section.

Study 2 plain: Notes

Pre-signs for separate parts of the arm in bar 2: upper arm (led by elbow) side low, lower arm (led by wrist) side high, ending with the arms crossed on the chest.

Carets for supports in bars 6–7, indicating that the feet remain where they are, but the sense of relationship changes as the torso tilts from a backward high direction to a forward high direction, the right leg straightens and the left leg bends to change the lunge from back to forward.

Foot hook in the final bar – a 'resultant touch', meaning that the ball of the right foot remains in contact with the floor after the left foot has stepped forward.

Study 2 (David Gordon): Notes

Contact bows and inclusion bows etc.

The bracket round the front surface of the chest symbol at the beginning indicates that the movement is initiated from that part – a 'passing state': i.e. just for that movement.

In bar 1, there are contact bows between palms and thighs (beat 3), and between hands and front surfaces of shoulder (bar 2, beat 3). In bar 6 the right hand touches the right side of the right knee – almost as if pushing the leg, although with no specific dynamic indication. In bar 10 both hands are placed on the left knee in the final position.

In bar 2, the bracket round the head movement is an inclusion bow, indicating that the movement extends a little into the neck and shoulders.

In bar 5, the bracket round the left support indicates that it is a partial support – the left foot is acting as two-thirds support, one-third gesture. This seems rather fiddly, but it shows that the support is not equally on both feet all the time – by the next beat the left foot has taken full support again, but during the manoeuvre as a whole it is the right foot that is constantly supporting in the full sense.

Also in that bar, the bracket linking to the rotation symbol for the right leg indicates that the rotation is a result of the previous movement. There has been a turn on the right foot, but without friction (as far as possible): i.e. keeping the foot anchored and turning the body above it (shown by the spot-hold), resulting in a turned-out foot.

The square bracket with the contraction sign round the arm gestures in bar 8 indicates that all the gestures should be one degree contracted.

Other assorted symbols

Bar 4: symbols at the side of the arms gestures in beat 2: these are known as 'track pins', and they allow for subtle intermediate directions. In this instance, the arms are both on a 'track' in front of but slightly across the body, so overlapping one another (but not touching, because one is higher than the other).

In bar 4, the symbol in the box indicates that the region from pelvis to ankles should be thought of as a unit during the following movements. The result is that the upper body stays facing the same direction, while the lower body rotates first one way, then the other. The foot hooks show which parts of the foot are in contact with the ground during these rotations.

Intermediate directions for gestures: as in the previous study – for example, in bar 5, beat 2–3, when the arms are a third of the way towards side high from side middle. So – a slightly high second position. Similarly at the beginning of the next bar; the arms are a third towards a diagonally forward middle direction from a side low direction. To find these positions, take the main position, and then move the arms a third of the way to the pin direction.

Centre of gravity/weight: in bar 8, the centre of gravity symbol is shown in the left body column, with a hold sign above. This indicates that, even though you rise to the ball of the foot during the step in low level, your centre of gravity should remain constant – in other words, your head stays the same height.

Fist – in bar 10, the symbol above the hand signs indicates a 'fist' – the hand is contracted both laterally and longitudinally.

Study 2: plain

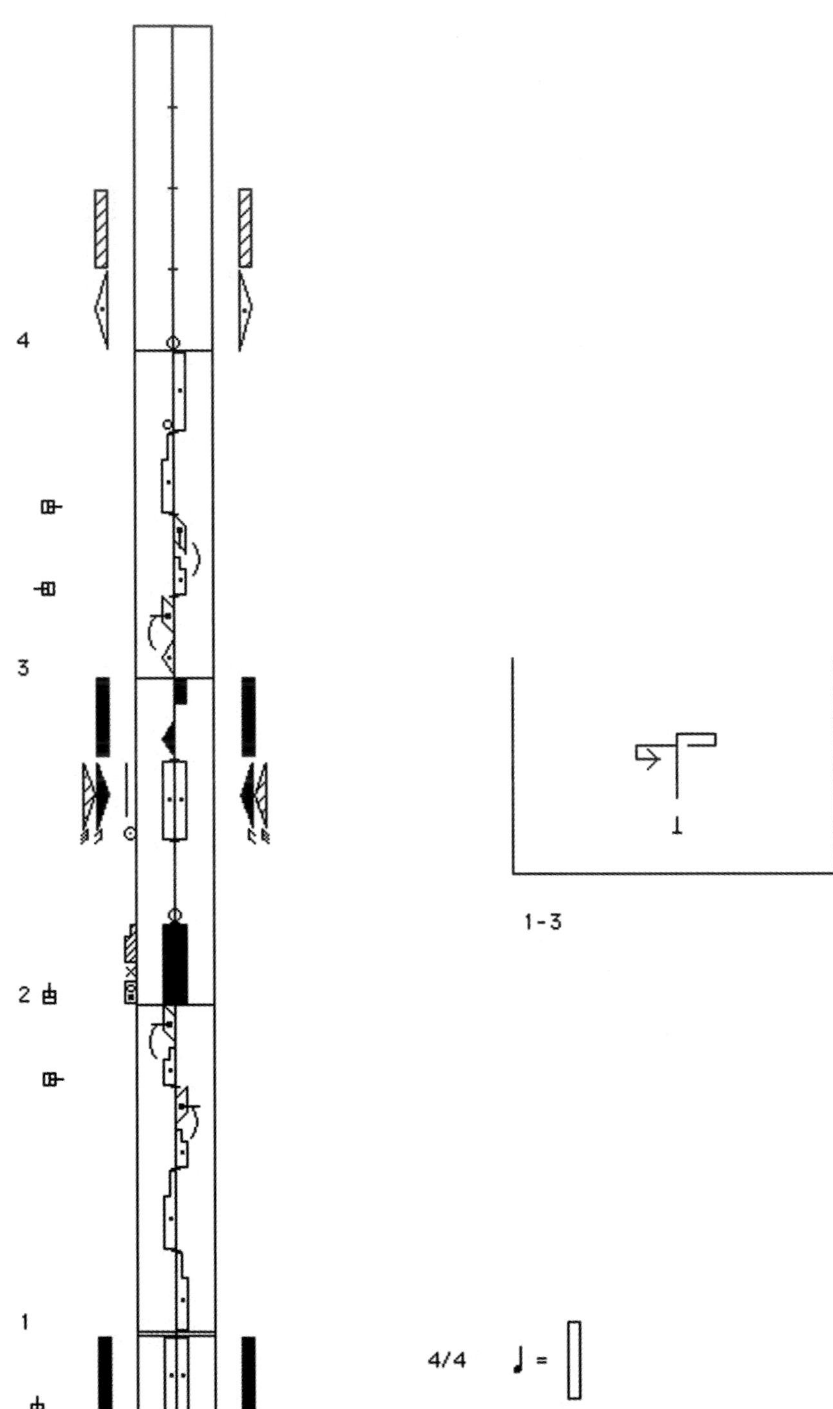

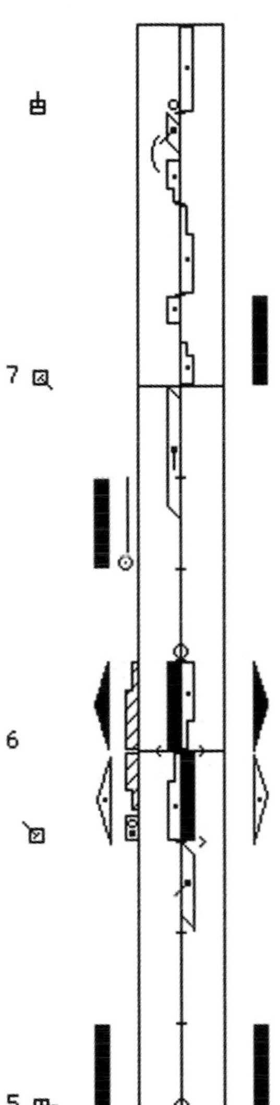

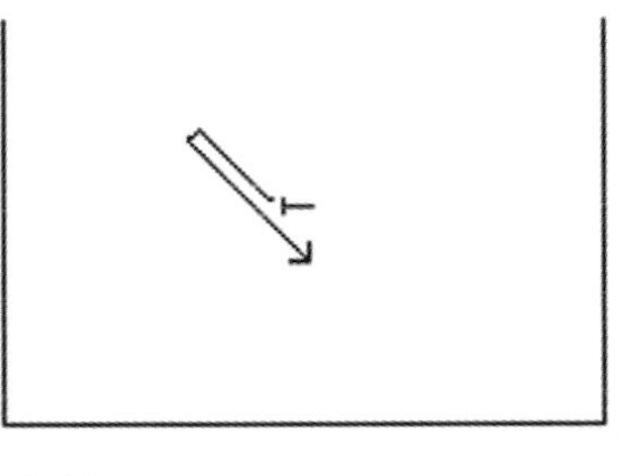

5-7

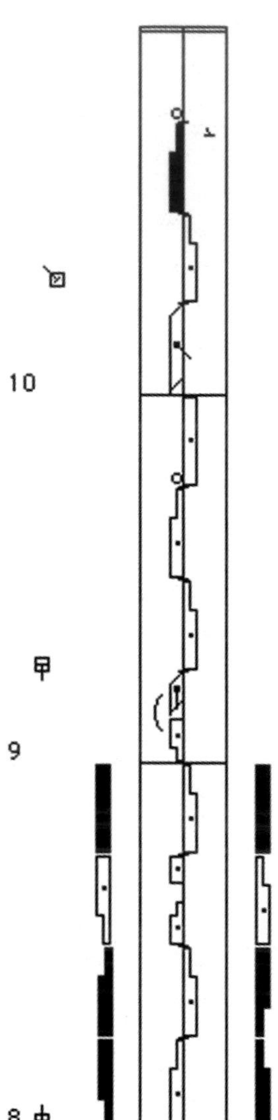

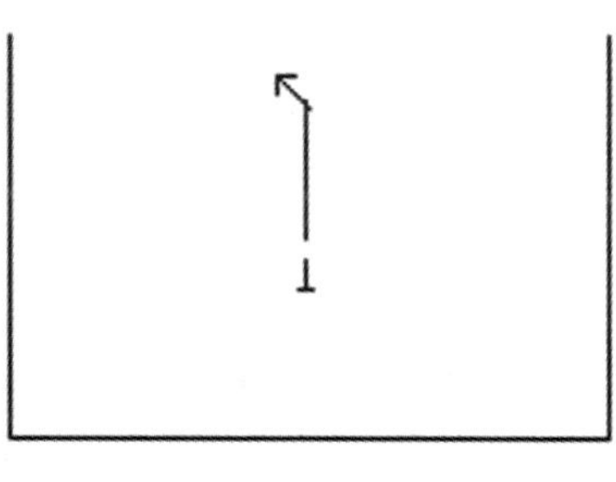
8-10

Study 2: (David Gordon)

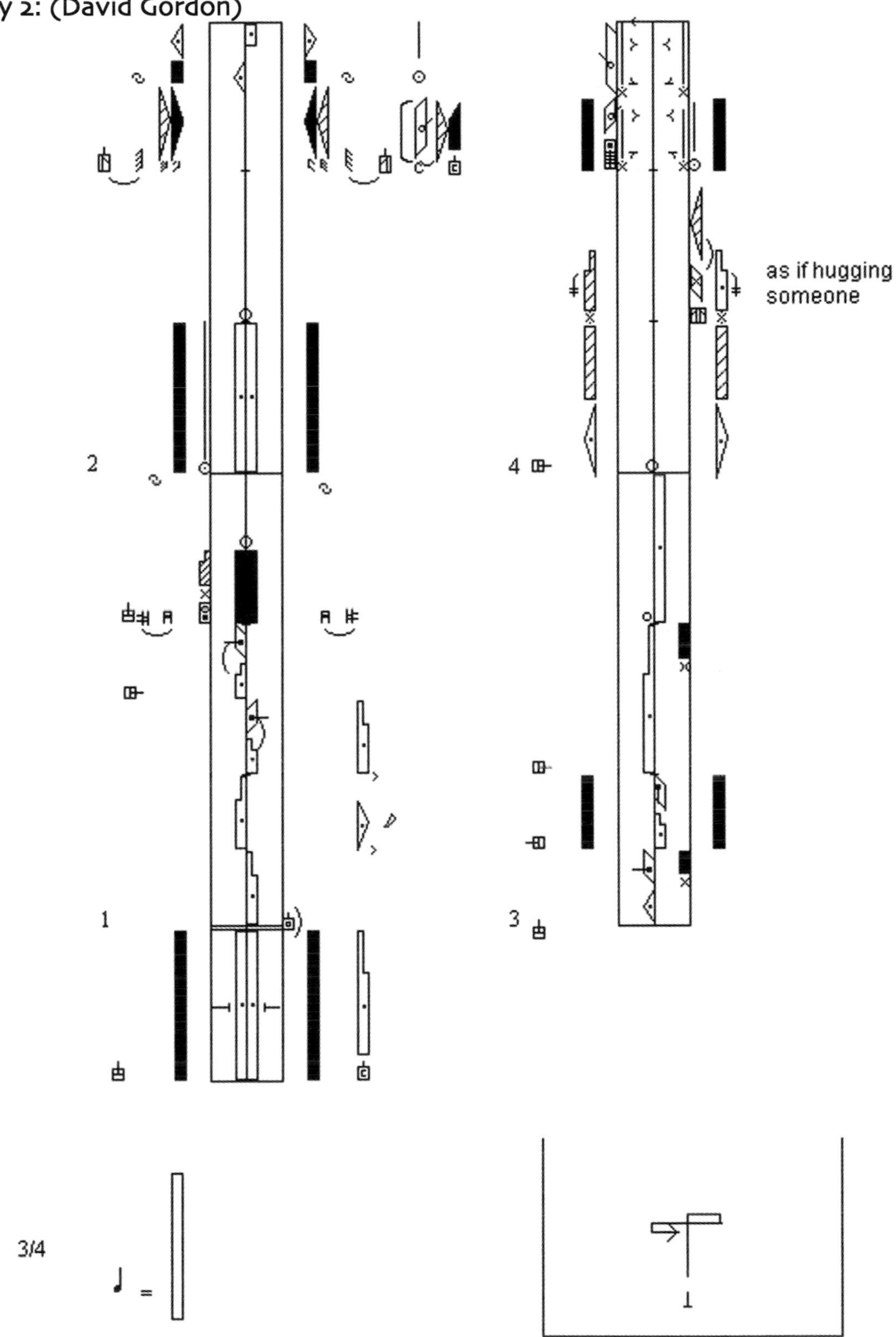

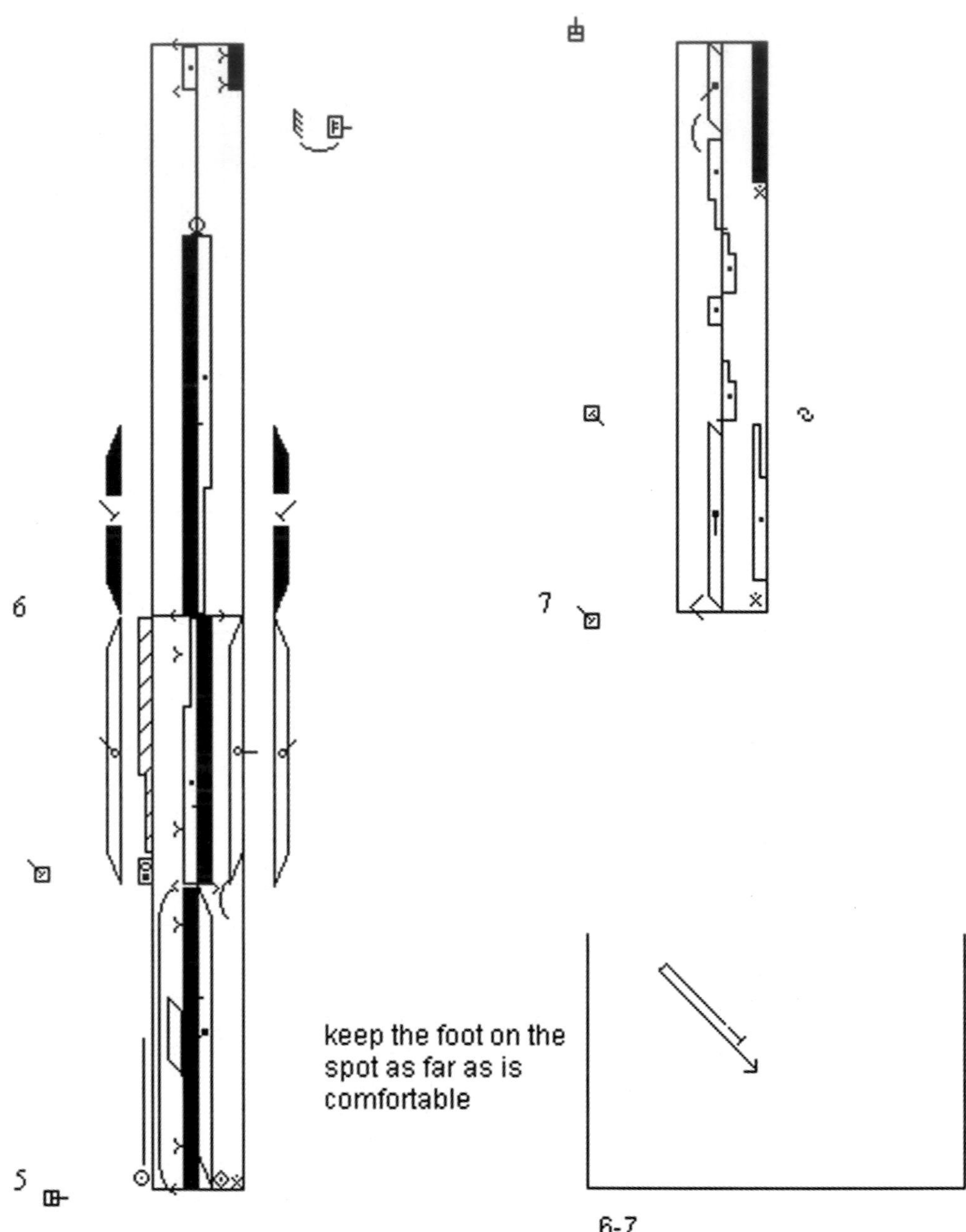
6
5
7
keep the foot on the spot as far as is comfortable
6-7

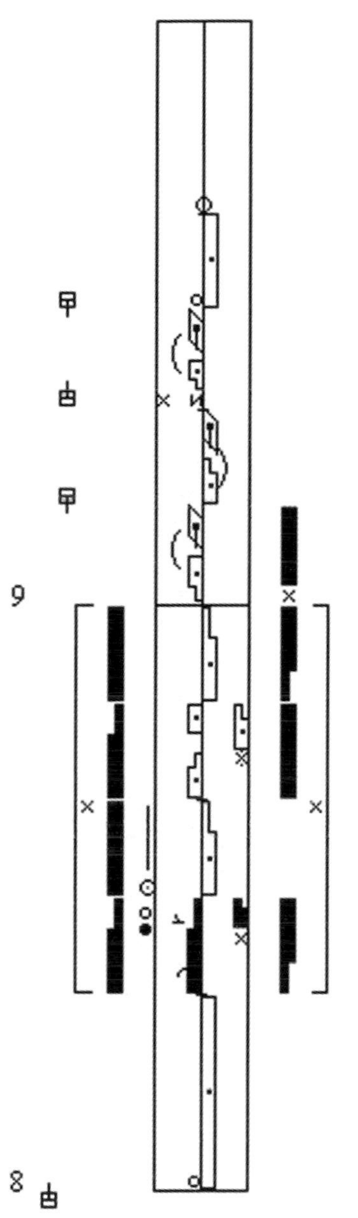

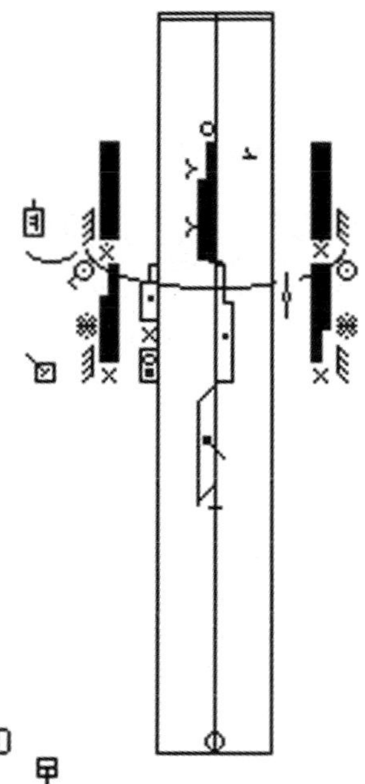

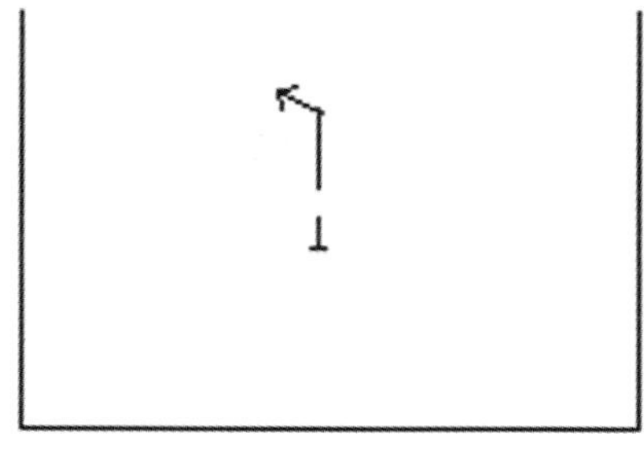

8-10

2

Martin Blain

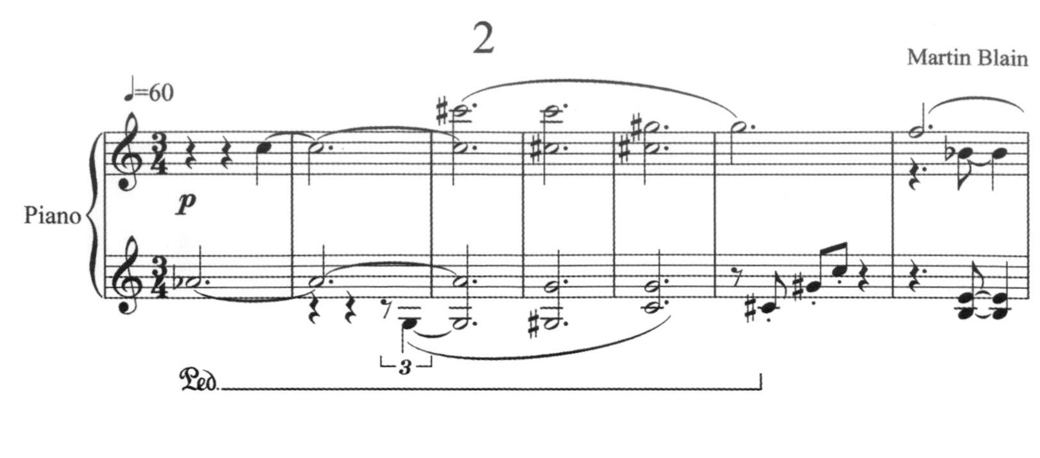

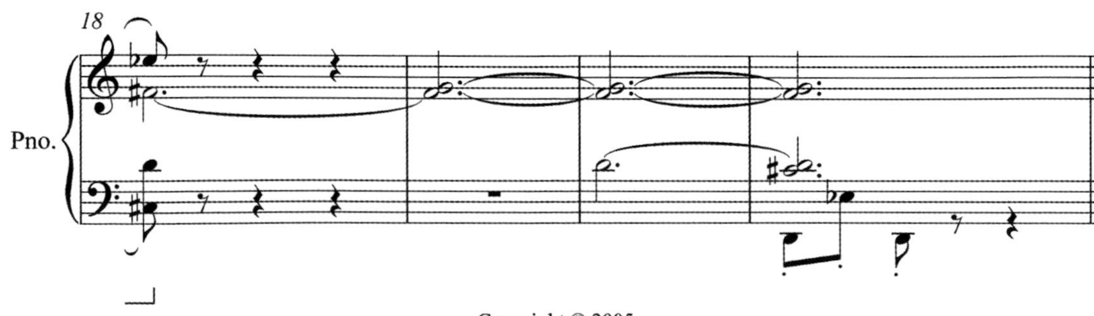

Other music suggestions

Title	Artist/composer	CD reference
Danksagung an den Bach (from *Die Schöne Müllerin*)	Franz Schubert	EMI Classics. 5.669072
Autumn Leaves	Ahmad Jamal	Chess GRP 18032
That's all	Ahmad Jamal	Chess GRP 18032
Nocturne in F sharp	Frederick Chopin	Naxos 8.550356
Chasing sheep is better left shepherds	Michael Nyman	*The Draughtsman's Contract* Virgin CASCD1158
Broadcasting from Home 5. White Mischief 10. Heartwind	Penguin Cafe Orchestra	Virgin EG Records EEGCD 38
Gnarly Buttons 1. Judah to Ocean	John Adams	*John's Book of Alleged Dances.* Kronos Quartet Nonesuch 7559 79465 2

Study 3

This study is based on ideas from the work of Jonathan Burrows. It could be seen in terms of a combination of pedestrian movement with a functional approach having hints of dramatic intention (e.g. through the use of focus and gesture). If it is performed with deliberate concentration and focus on each movement for its own sake, it could take on something of the dramatic effects of a work such as *Stoics* (1991) or *Very* (1992): seeming to tell a story, but never making that story explicit. The choice of music can make a big difference, too; sometimes Burrows works with a score that creates an interesting or humorous disjunction with the dance, such as in *Stoics*, where the middle character is lifted and carried with great deliberation and not much dignity, to the strains of the *Blue Danube Waltz* by Johann Strauss the Younger. On a number of more recent works, Burrows has collaborated with composer Matteo Fargion, and has spoken of the idea of 'holes' in the music that allow the dance to be seen through them and vice versa[3], which suggests a different music–dance relationship.

The study begins and ends with the dancer's focus directed toward the upstage right corner, at a high level, with both hands placed on the left hip. Apart from this sense of returning, the movements do not suggest any particular development – rather, they tend to be quite distinct from each other. There is a little repetition (bar 3), but in both cases it occurs immediately after the initial presentation of the motif, and does not develop any further. The rhythmic patterns of motifs is not regular, and the phrase overall is punctuated by pauses, creating a slightly disjointed effect. There are a few gestures that suggest significance, such as the opening position of hands on hip, the clenched fists and flexed foot (bar 3), reminding us of the possibility of character or situation, even though these things are never made explicit. There are some movements in the lower torso, for example the circling pelvis (bar 1) and the twisting jumps (bar 3), as well as tilts and contractions of the whole torso or chest. However, none of these is repeated enough, arguably, to look like a characteristic feature or motif in its own right. The spatial design of the phrase as a whole is angular and contained within a relatively small performance area, giving some sense of introversion to the whole study.

Choreographers to experiment with:

- William Forsythe – perhaps with more extreme gestures, or some reference to *danse d'école* (*Solo*, *Steptext*)
- Lloyd Newson – probably involving partner work, especially contact and supported work, and more clearly defined characterisation and setting, with use of props (*Never Again*, *Enter Achilles*)
- Yolande Snaith – potentially involving more developed characterisation, and perhaps with costume and props being particularly important (*Should Accidentally Fall*, *Gorgeous Creatures*)
- Mats Ek – again, perhaps with more developed characterisation, and with deeper *pliés*, higher extensions, larger movements.

Further information on these choreographers included at the end of this section.

[3] Duerden, R. (2001), 'Jonathan Burrows: Exploring the frontiers', *Dancing Times*, March, pp. 551–7.

Study 3 plain: Notes

Space hold in bar 4 – indicates that the turn on the left foot should be 'frictionless', i.e. the foot does not move, but the body rotates above it. The foot will end up 'turned out' in the following lunge position.

Change of supports in bar 9 – at beat 2 the legs bend to the maximum, so that the dancer ends in a squat; then the weight is taken on the hips (sitting on the floor), with the feet still on the floor (indicated by the foot-hooks, showing the whole foot in contact with the floor). The support then changes to the back surface of the torso – so the dancer ends lying on the floor, arms out to the side, legs bent.

In bar 10, the centre of gravity is shown to move to high level, which is the 'normal' state for it, when standing – so this indicates that the dancer stands up again, via a *plié* and then straightening the legs. The description of this phrase is minimal – so the dancer has some scope for finding the easiest way of achieving the drop to the floor and the recovery. In the complex version of this study, there is considerably more detail included, but here you can more easily see the general idea.

Study 3 (Jonathan Burrows): Notes

Track pins in the starting position – in this case, each foot is directly under its own hip, rather than right next to the other foot.

Contact bows: the starting position shows the hands both on the left hip (compare the ending position, too). The right hand is on top of the left, shown by the white pin at the side of the hand symbol.

In bar 2, the bows in the leg gesture columns indicate that the rotation of the legs which follows occurs as a result of the previous movement (c.f. Study 2).

In bar 3 there is a dotted line bow connecting left wrist to right knee – this means that the body parts come near each other but do not actually touch.

In bar 4, the double bows extending out from the hands indicate a sliding movement of the hands on the floor, as the body lowers to a lying position, and again as the dancer rises to a sitting position. Notice also the dotted lines at the side of the arm gestures after this, indicating a 'passive' movement – the arms fall naturally to place low as the dancer sits up.

Design drawing: the rather lovely pattern to the left of the staff in bar 1 is a design drawing. It shows pictorially the pattern made by a body-part in space. In this instance it is the pelvis describing a circular path (start at the 'blob' end of the shape in between the arrows). The symbol directly underneath this indicates that the pattern is 'drawn' on an imaginary surface below the pelvis (shown by the colour of the pin). The extension symbol to the left means that the shape should be large!

Body key: in bars 3 and 4, the star-like shape before the arm gestures is a 'body key'. This indicates that the gestures should be read from the perspective of the body – what it feels like.

To find the positions, take them in a standing position, and then tilt the body as indicated, keeping the arms in the same bodily relationship. They 'feel' side high and side low in relation to the body, but to the observer they look quite different.

Changing supports: in bar 4 there are indications for the centre of gravity and the supports, which are different from the rest. The centre of gravity drops as the knees bend to a squat; the supports change to the hips half-way through beat 2 (sitting), with the feet flat on the floor, legs bent. The next support is the back surface of the torso (beat 3) and the torso tilts to backward middle, moving successionally. So the step back on the left foot at the beginning of the bar leads into a drop to the floor to a sitting position, then rolling down the spine, sliding the arms out to the sides *en route*. The torso recovers to place high, and the support become the hips again – so, the dancer rises to a sitting position. Then, bending the legs even more, the weight shifts to the left foot, then to both feet, and the dancer rises to standing. All in the space of a single bar!

Study 3: plain

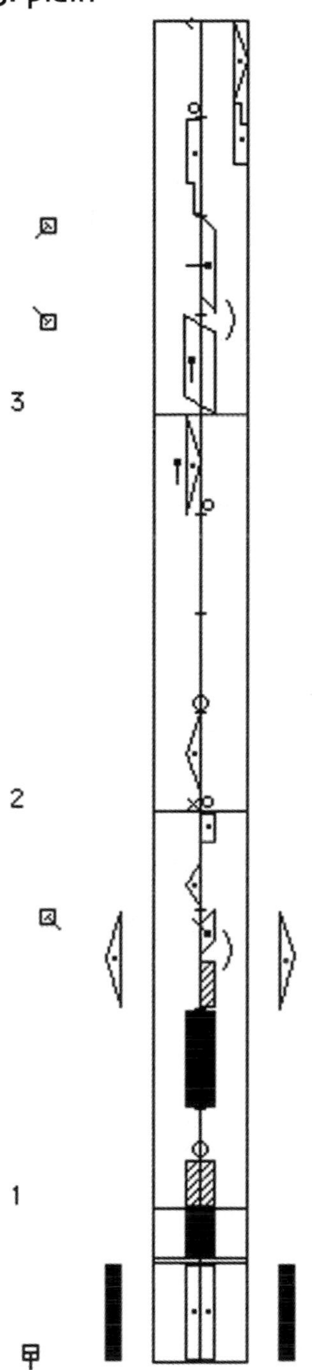

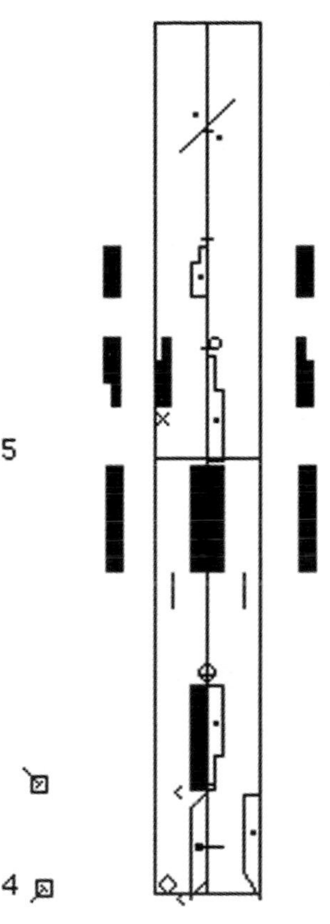

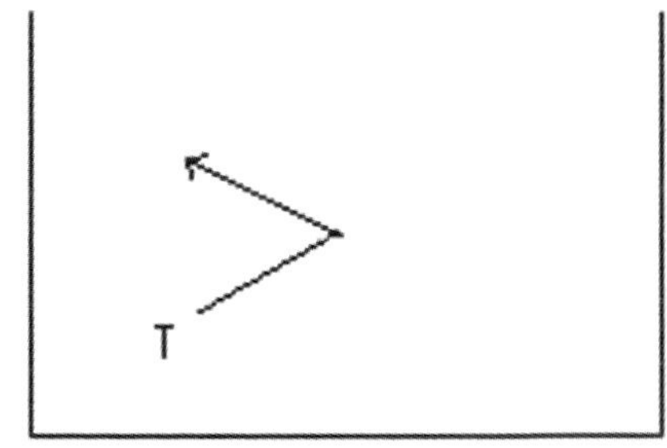

1-5

4/4 ♩ =

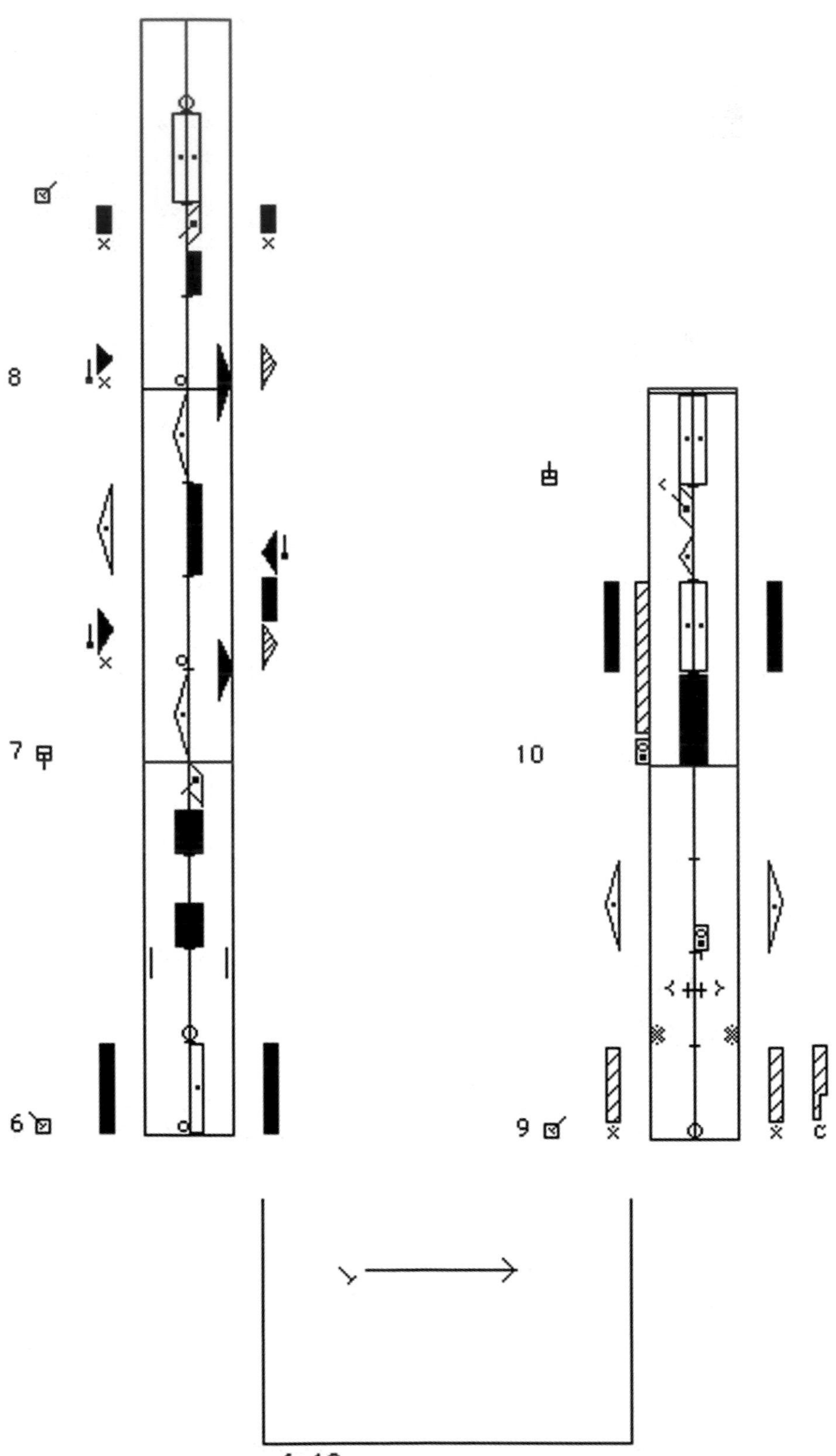
8
7
6
10
9
C
6-10

Study 3: (Jonathan Burrows)

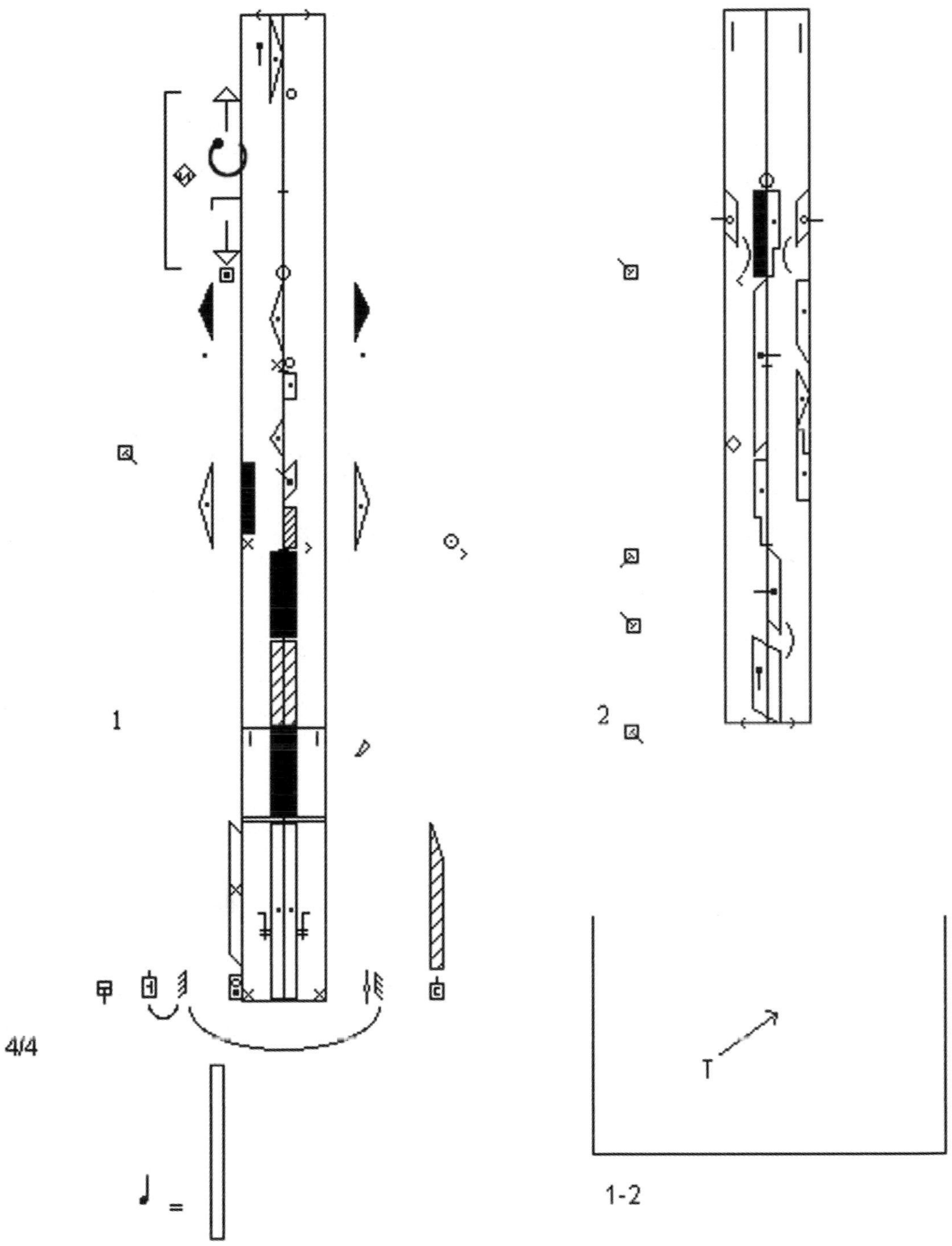

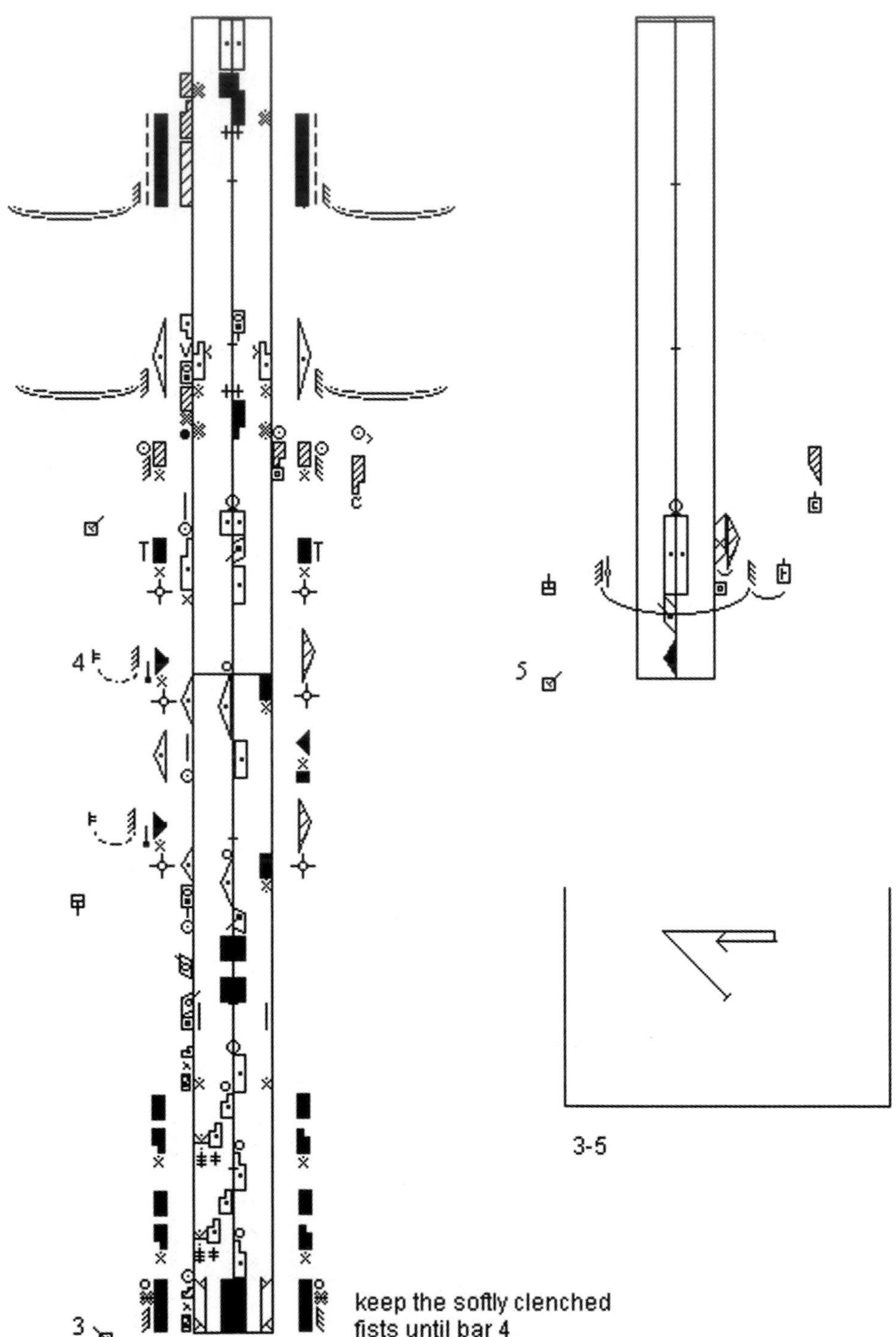
4
5
3
keep the softly clenched
fists until bar 4
3-5

3

Martin Blain

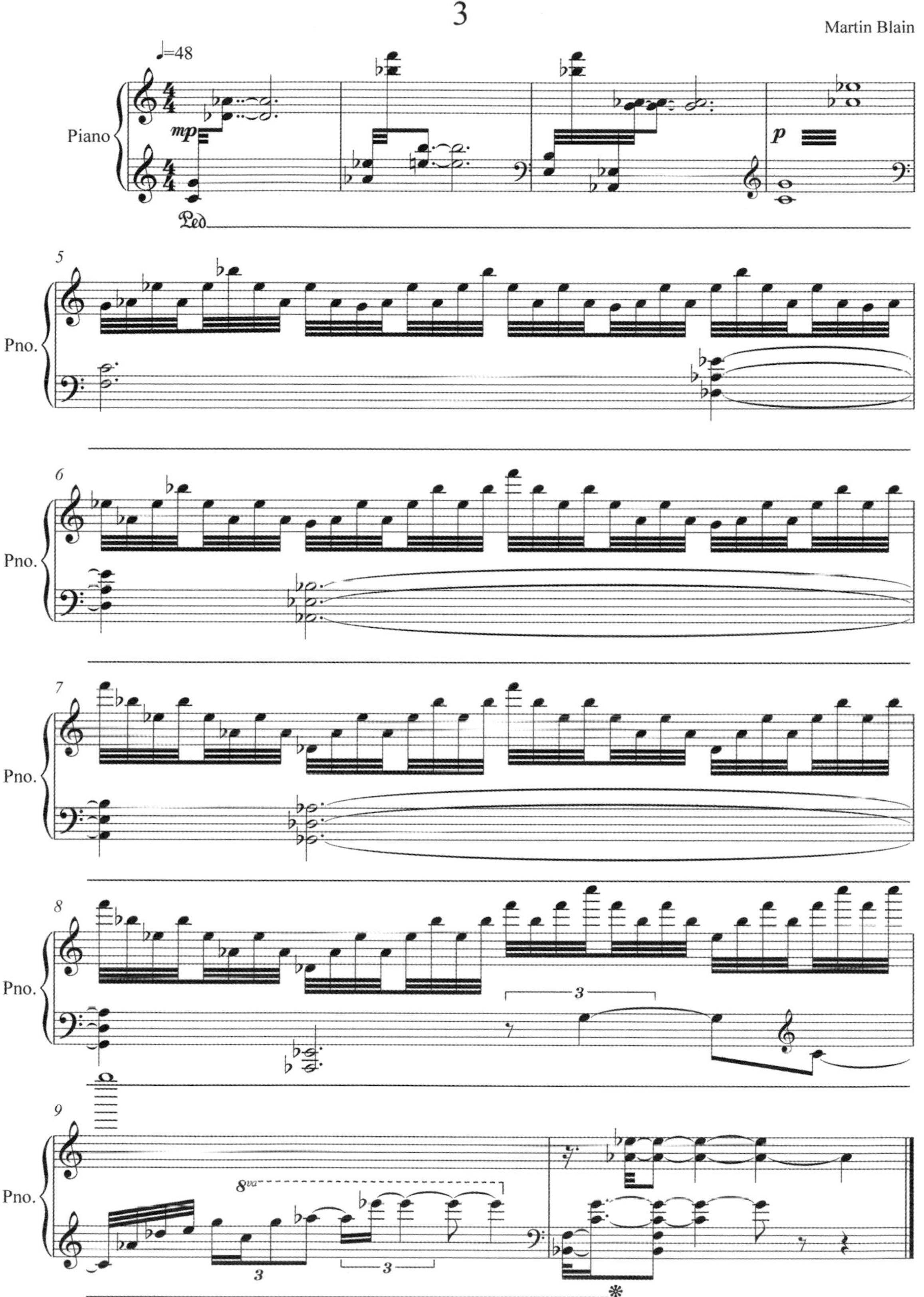

Other music suggestions

Title	Artist/composer	CD reference
Misterioso	Thelonius Monk	Fantasy OJCCD 206-2
Night Club 1960	Astor Piazzolla	EMI 5.679432
Robotts	Huns/Bartoff/Schneider	*Possessed* Mute Records CD STUMM 111
Romance in A Minor	Clara Schumann	Naxos 8.553501
Tabula Rasa: Ludus	Arvo Pärt	Naxos 8.554591
You make me feel so young	Frank Sinatra	Capitol Records CDP7465702
Gnarly Buttons 2. Toot Nipple 8. Hammer & Chisel	John Adams	*John's Book of Alleged Dances.* Kronos Quartet Nonesuch 7559 79465 2
Broadcasting from Home 5. White Mischief	Penguin Cafe Orchestra	Virgin EG Records EEGCD 38
Kronos Caravan 3. Aaj Ki Raat (Rahul Dev Burman)	Kronos Quartet	Nonesuch 7559 79490 2

Study 4

This study draws from the work of Mark Morris, focusing on a few characteristics of his style, especially the use of gesture, combined or in conjunction with sweeping pathways and full use of the body. Morris has made many choreographies involving character and action, such as *The Hard Nut* (1991) and *Dido and Aeneas* (1989), and many that have no specific characters or setting but hint at these things, especially through gestural movements that draw attention to the dancer as an individual. In all his work, music is of prime importance, and he frequently bases his choreography on structural and dynamic aspects of the music at different levels (for example in *L'Allegro, Il Penseroso ed Il Moderato*, 1988). His movement vocabulary ranges quite widely, drawing on influences from different theatrical and folk or social dance forms. It does not often highlight technical expertise, and can include pedestrian movement, although it is clearly demanding on the dancers in terms of energy, stamina and dynamic versatility.

A generous use of space characterises this study, which incorporates both straight and circular pathways with a defined focus – not meandering or vague. The structure is clearly framed by the gentle walking phrase, turning on a straight path, which appears at the beginning and at the end; apart from this, there is little or no repetition in the movement itself. The whole body is involved, with twists, tilts and contractions in the torso, for example in the deep lunge in bar 4. An important characteristic feature is the use of evocative gesture – which may be grandiose and sweeping (e.g. bars 5–6), small and inscrutable (e.g. the head movements in bar 10) or dramatically sculptural (e.g. arms in bar 9).

Choreographers to experiment with:

- Jiri Kylian – perhaps making this a duet, increasing the dynamic range, altering or maybe playing down some of the gestures (*Transfigured Night*, *Sarabande*)
- Paul Taylor – the speed and dynamic could be altered to create different effects, gesture could be made more or less specific, with incorporation of leaps and faster travelling sequences (*Roses*, *Esplanade*)
- Pina Bausch – the phrase might be fragmented, interspersed with more pedestrian movement, accompanied by spoken text, music or silence; props and set could play a significant role (*Café Muller*, *The Window Cleaner*)
- Siobhan Davies – consider working very closely with your dancers, their movement styles and preferences, and incorporating these (*White Man Sleeps*, *Birdsong*).

Further information on these choreographers is included at the end of this section.

Study 4 plain: Notes

Parts of limbs: starting position for the right arm indicates separate directions and levels for the upper and lower arm, as in Study 2; also the leg gesture in bar 7 and the arm gesture in bar 12.

The opening phrase incorporates walking on a straight path, rotating around the dancer's own axis. The wavy line in the middle of the staff is an 'ad lib' sign – indicating that the walking steps have no set timing or number of steps.

Foot-hooks: several times you will see a foot-hook in the leg gesture column without a direction symbol attached (bars 4, 6, 8 and 11). This is when it is a 'resultant touch' – i.e. the foot touches the floor (ball of foot or toe, in these cases) as a result of the previous step on the other foot. It is 'left behind' by the step, in other words.

The small 'v' symbols in front of arm gestures in bars 6 and 7 indicate a successional movement through the limb.

In bar 6, notice also that the right arm, after its successional movement to a straight position forward middle, contracts and then extends again.

Study 4 (Mark Morris): Notes

Contact, inclusion, and 'passing state' bows: in bars 4, 17 and 18 there is a dotted-line bow connecting body parts. This indicates that the parts come close, but do not touch.

The brackets round arm gestures in bar 7 (slightly square, but with rounded 'corners') are inclusion bows, indicating the inclusion of the shoulder in the arm movement.

At the end of bar 5 into bar 6 there are two sets of bows. The outer one includes the symbol for heel of hand, indicating that the movement within the bracket as a whole is led by this body part (see also bars 15–16: gesture led by thumb side of wrist). The inner, smaller bow, including a black pin, indicates a deviation – on the way to forward diagonal high, the arms 'deviate' downwards, producing a kind of 'scooping' movement.

Intermediate directions: in bars 8 and 9, gestures are modified by the placement of pins inside the direction symbols. In bar 6, the white pin indicates that the arm gesture is a third of the way towards side high, from side middle; in bar 9 the white pins indicates that the facing of the palms is a third towards place high from forward high.

Rotation symbols are attached to some gestures – they are small, and apply only to the particular gesture (bars 5–6 and 9).

Track pins also appear – in bar 9, indicating that the arms are directly in line with each vertically (one above the other).

Ad lib signs etc: the ad lib symbol (wavy line) inside the staff indicates that the number and exact timing of the steps is left to the dancer to decide. The shorter, more acutely wavy version in bar 10 for the head is similar, but indicates a series of deviations to forward high (indicated by the white pin) and back (back to normal symbol). So – a nodding movement, in free timing.

Successional and approaching movements: the small 'v' in front of a gesture indicates a successional movement through the limb to the finishing position. Similar, but on a larger scale, is the elongated 'v' in bars 15–16 – like a musical *crescendo* sign but standing up. It means movement towards, or approaching. Here, it is the face that begins looking side low, and gradually changes to looking side high the other way.

Notice also the occasional contraction signs in the leg gesture column, indicating slightly bent legs; also some arm gestures, and some contracting and extending of the arms using these symbols with actions strokes (bars 6, 7, 8 and 12).

Effort symbols: in bars 7 and 8 the symbol at the far right of the staff indicates a 'pressing' quality in the movement. 'Effort' symbols in notation give dynamic indications that help to understand different qualities of movement.

Study 4: plain

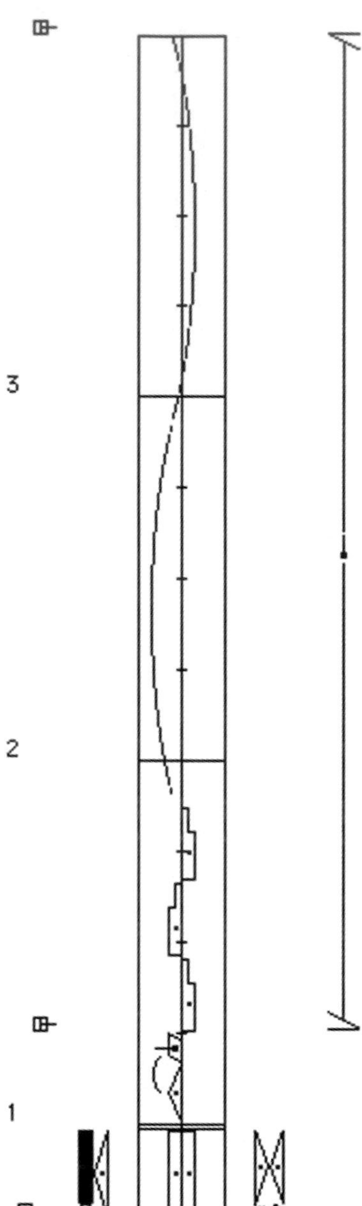

4/4 ♩ =

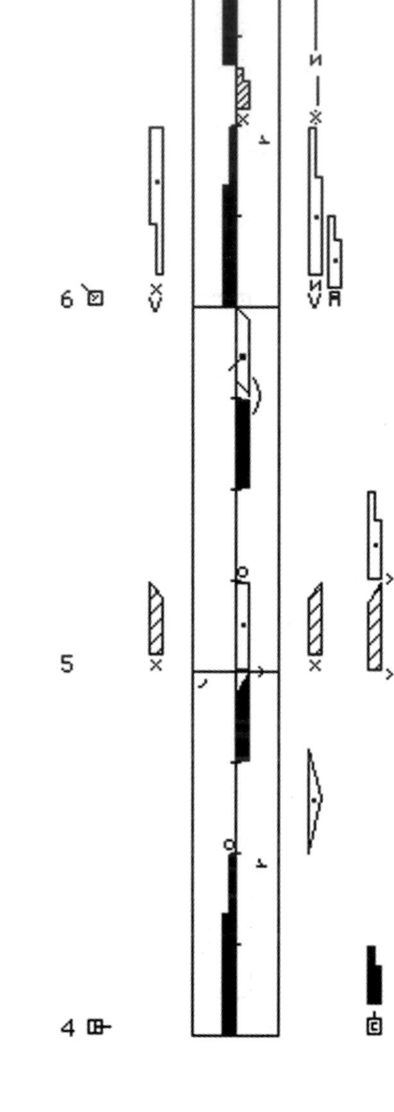

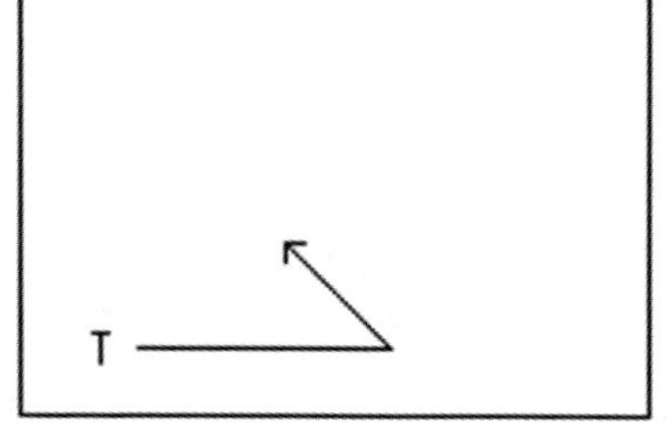

1-6

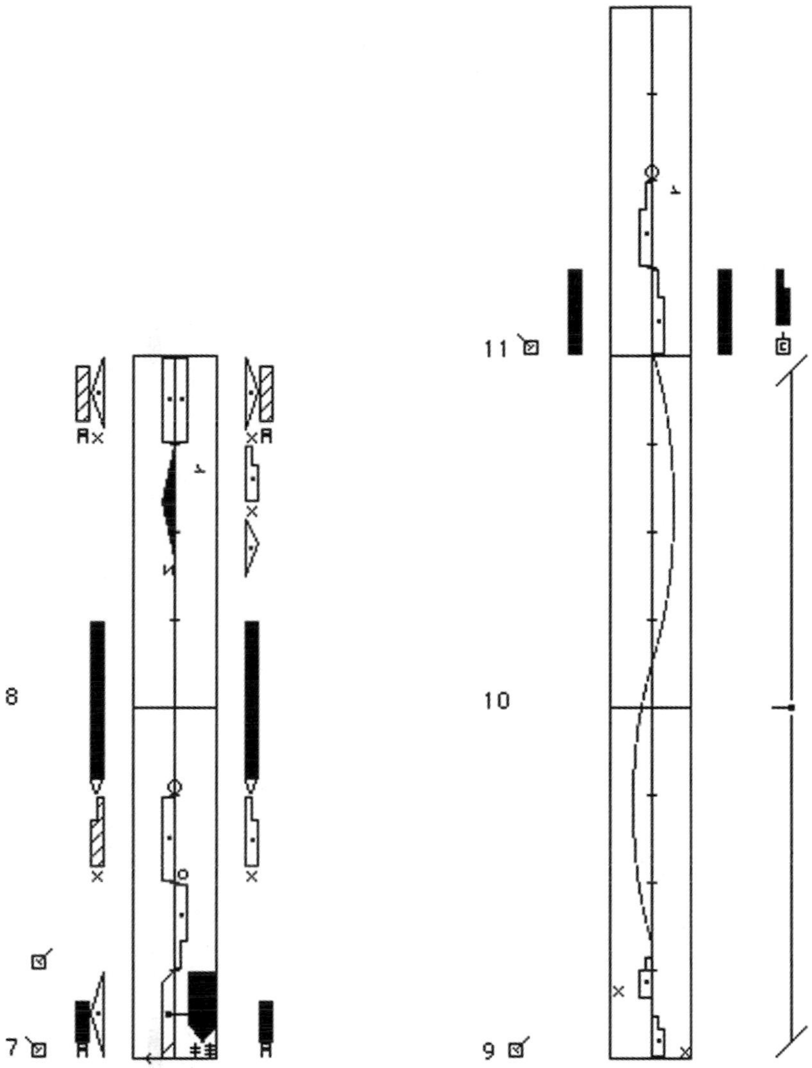

11

8

10

7

9

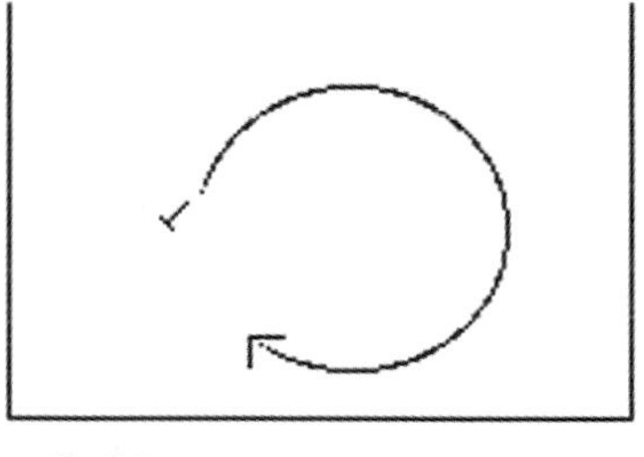

9-10

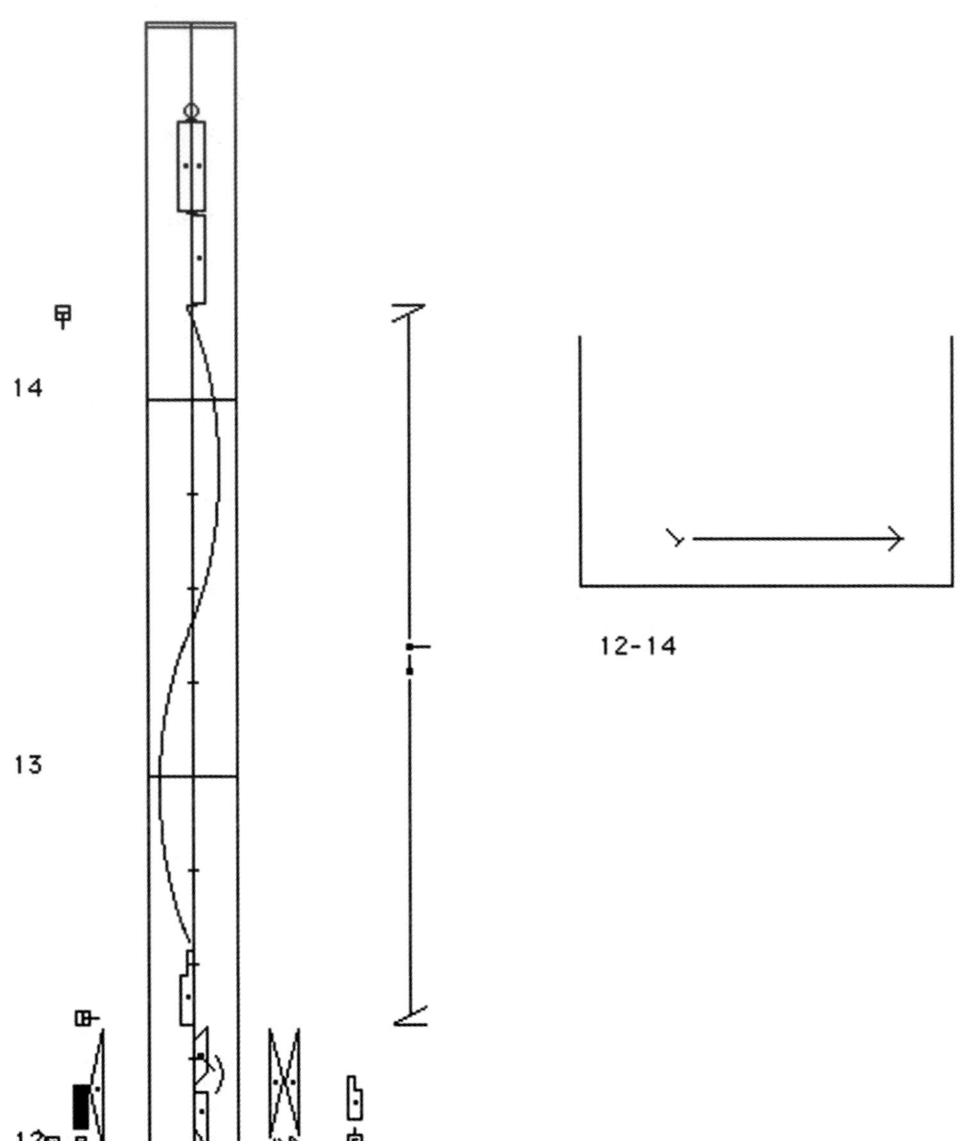
14
13
12
12-14

Study 4: (Mark Morris)

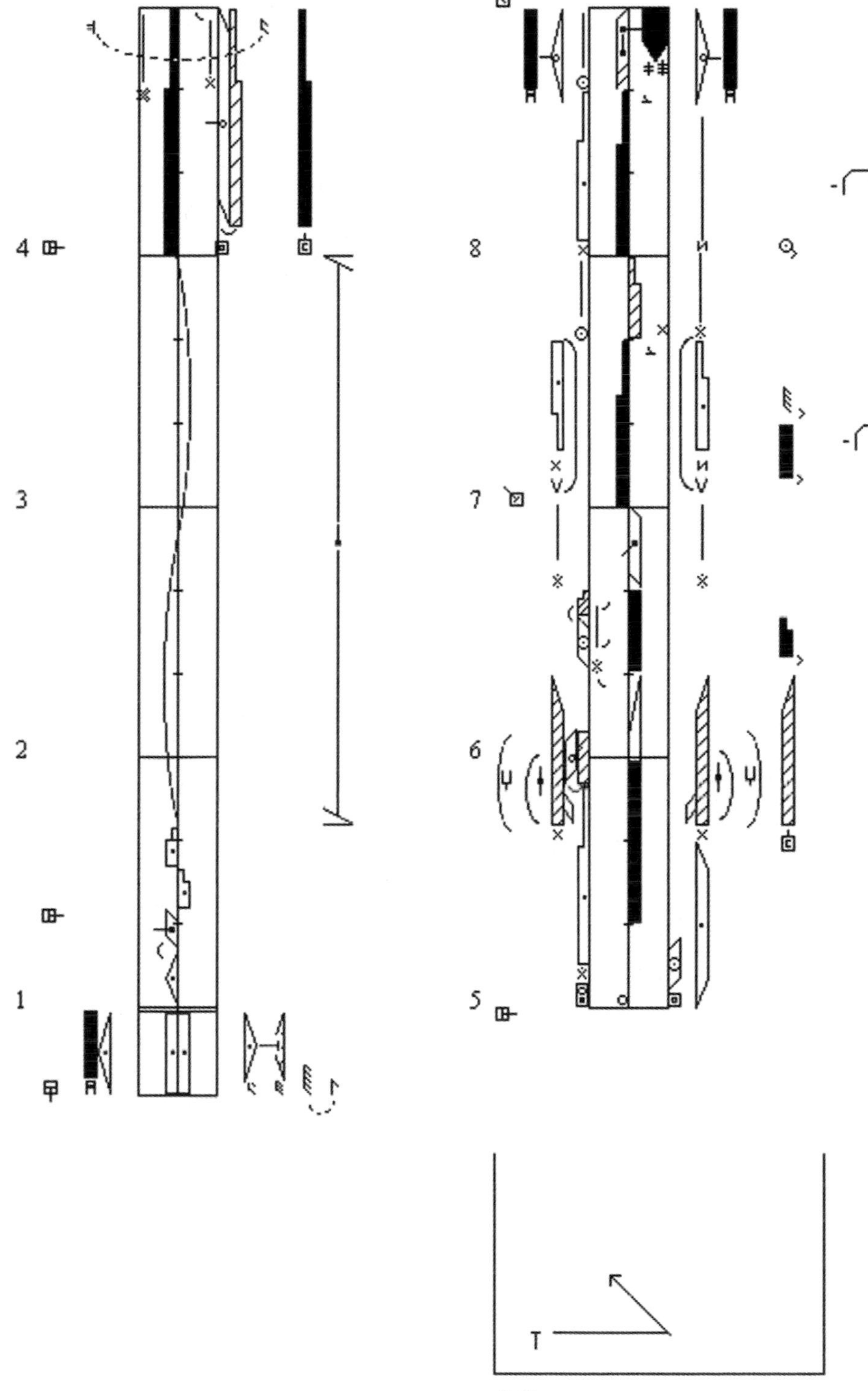

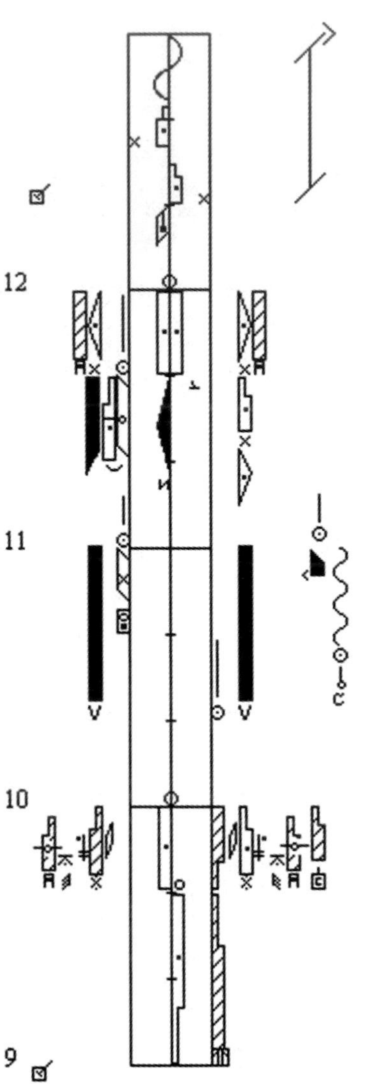

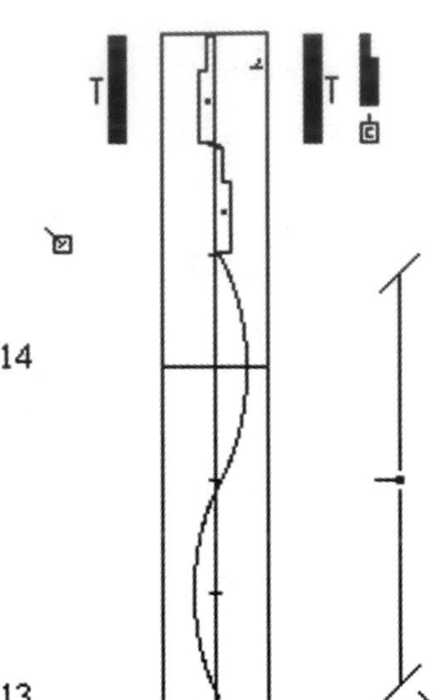

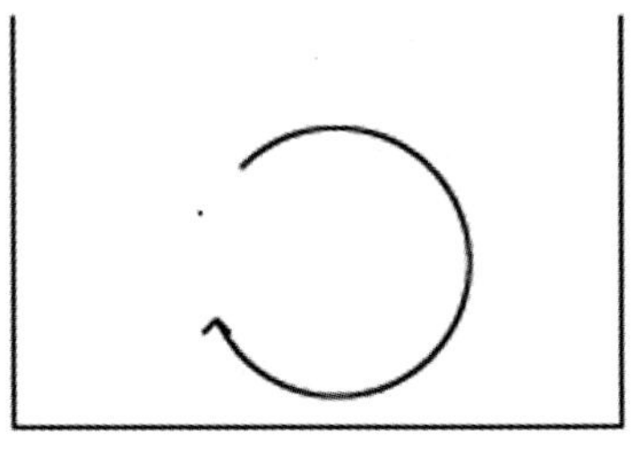

12-14

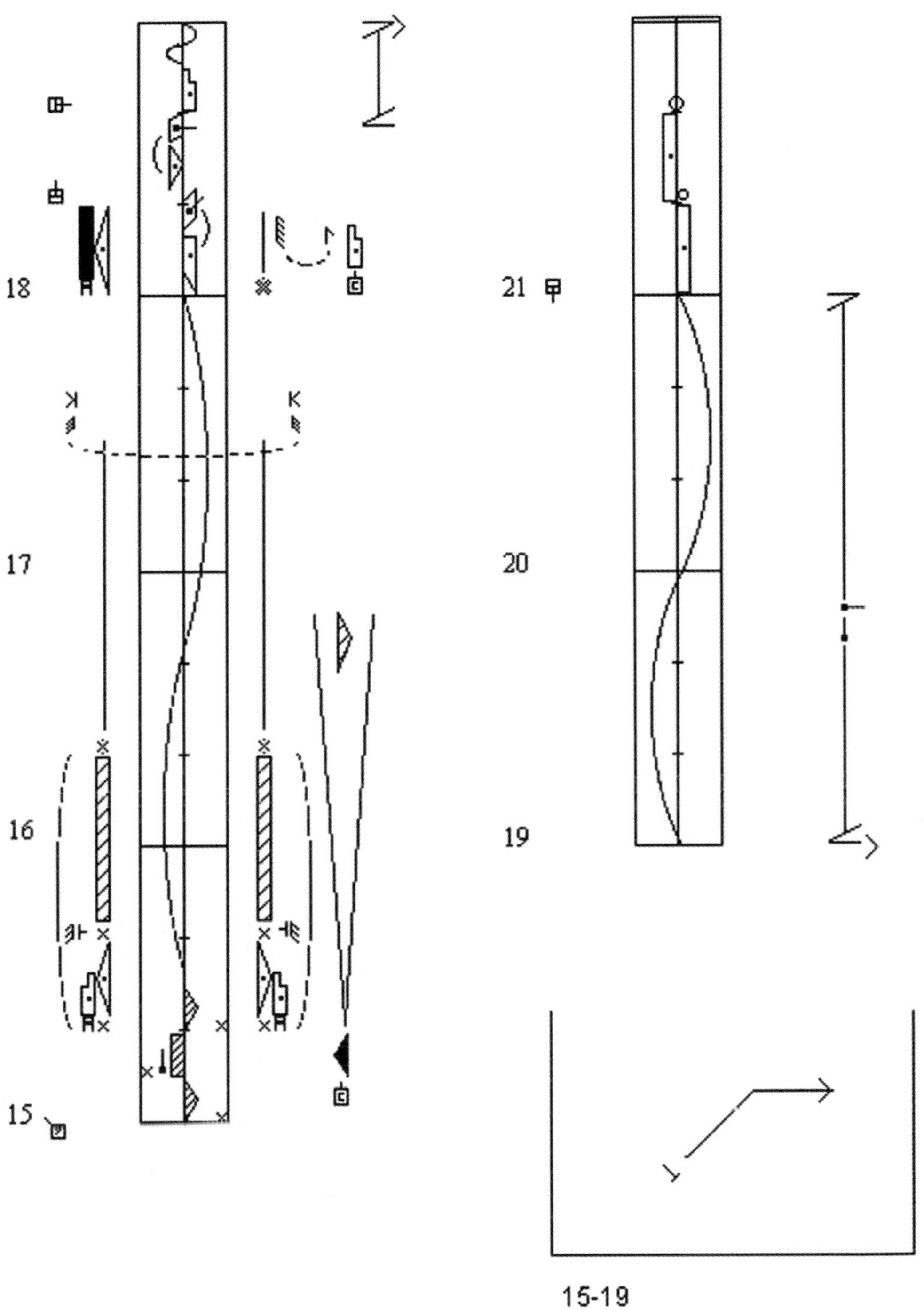

18
17
16
15
21
20
19
15-19

4

Martin Blain

2

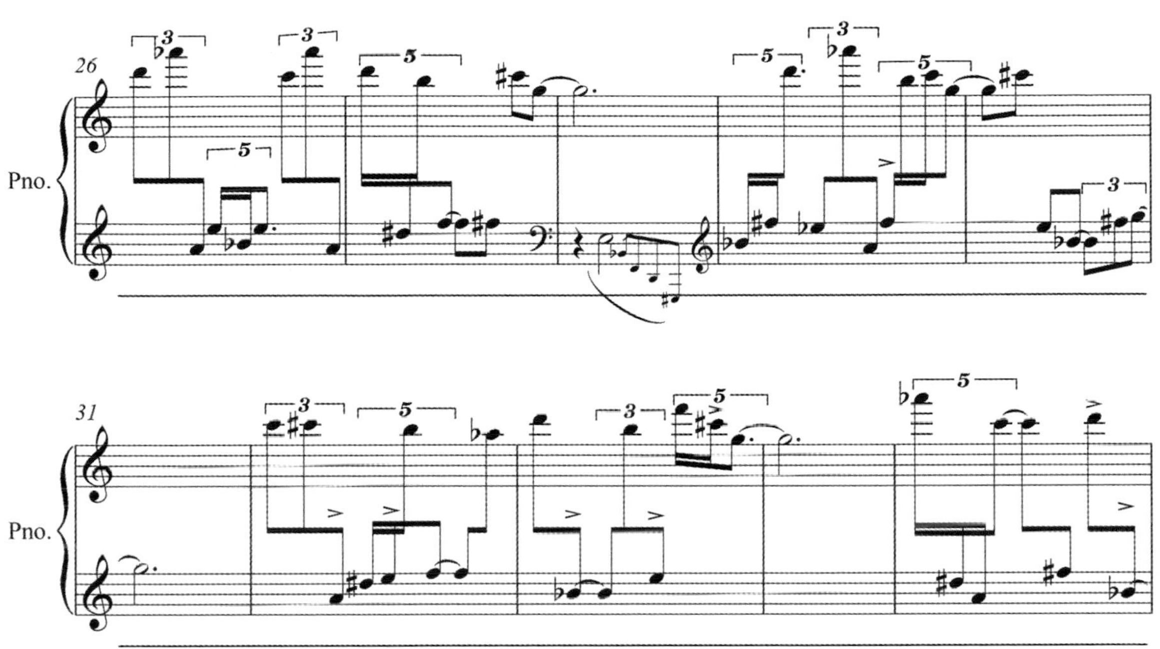

Other music suggestions

Title	Artist/composer	CD reference
Prelude Op. 11 no. 3	Alexander Scriabin	ASV CD DCA 919
The Archangel Trip	Gavin Bryars	*Short Cuts* Argo 443 396-2
Desert of Roses	Robert Moran	*Short Cuts* Argo 443 396-2
Will you still love me tomorrow?	Carole King	Tapestry EPC32110
Dance no. 1 (*In the Upper Room*)	Philip Glass	*Dance Pieces* Sony MK39539

Study 5

This study does not draw on any particular choreographer for influence, but is characterised by its sweep and flow, suspension and use of gravity in different ways. The focus is chiefly directed towards the gestural patterns of the arms, but the supports and, in particular, the body movements (in 5b) complement the arms and reinforce the sense of flow.

The addition of more complex stepping patterns, or the involvement of different body parts, could alter the overall feel of this study very considerably. It has the potential to be developed into either a dramatic or an abstract study.

Choreographers to experiment with:

— Siobhan Davies (*White Man Sleeps, Birdsong*)
— Pina Bausch (*Café Muller, 1980*)
— Trisha Brown – using her 'cube' idea, or accumulation technique
— Paul Taylor – with or without characterisation (*Airs, Tango Piazzolla, Last Look*)
— Mark Morris – ditto (*The Hard Nut, Dido and Aeneas, Gloria*)
— William Tuckett – ditto (*Duet for the Betterment of A*)
— Kenneth Macmillan – perhaps in the context of a dramatic duet (*Romeo and Juliet, Mayerling, Winter Dreams, The Judas Tree*)
— Lloyd Newson – ditto (*Never Again, Enter Achilles, Strange Fish*)
— Akram Khan – experimenting with movement dynamic (*Fall*)
— Wayne McGregor – incorporating more involvement of the torso, more extreme extensions, etc. (*Chrysalis*).

Further information on these choreographers is included at the end of this section.

Study 5 plain: Notes

Successional movements – notice the small 'v' in front of some of the arm gestures, indicating a successional movement through the limb.

Parts of limbs: in bars 4 and 5 the upper and lower arms are notated individually.

Palm facings: in bars 7 and 8 the palm facings are indicated; the caret symbols show that the following facings also apply to the palms – so turn the hands accordingly during this phrase.

Study 5 (Gestural study): Notes

Centre of gravity or centre of weight: the straight pin above the centre of gravity symbol in bar 1 indicates a 'deviation' forwards – in other words, there is a feeling of shifting the weight slightly forwards, as if about to fall, and then catching it again in the subsequent movement.

Contact bows: the dotted line (bar 4) indicates that the parts come close but do not touch. In bar 6 the hand touches the front of the shoulder and maintains that touch (via the hold sign) until the 'release' sign at the end of the bar. The contact bow swung between palm and back of the hand in bar 7 also has a spot hold and a hold sign above that, indicating that the contact should be maintained throughout this phrase of movement, until cancelled by the 'zed' caret in the next bar.

The study ends with a buoyant dynamic, indicated in the symbol at the right-hand side of the staff.

This study is notated as if in 3/4 time, although the music is scored in 9/8 and 6/8. Keep the pulse steady, and let the dance phrase ride with the music.

Study 5: plain

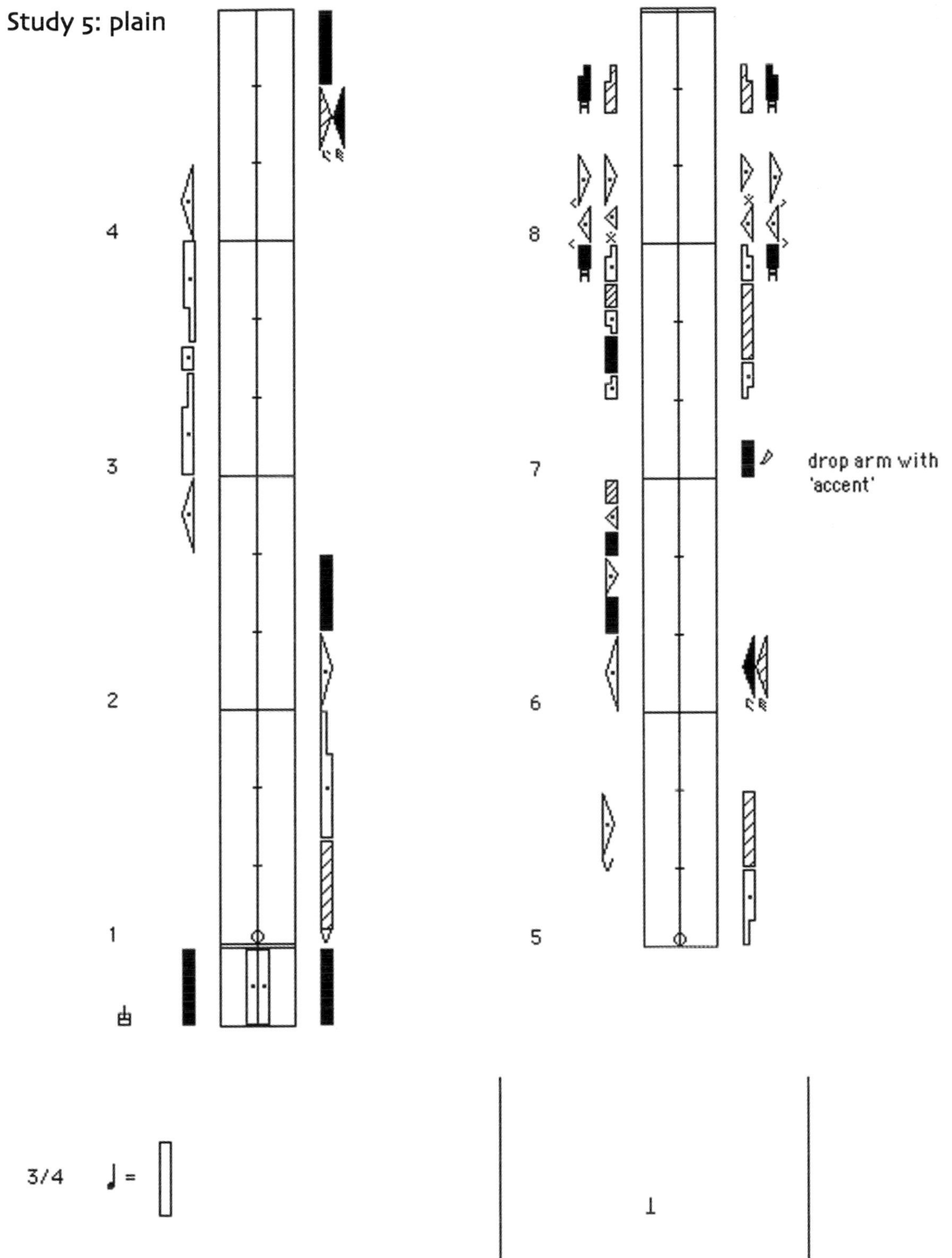

Study 5a

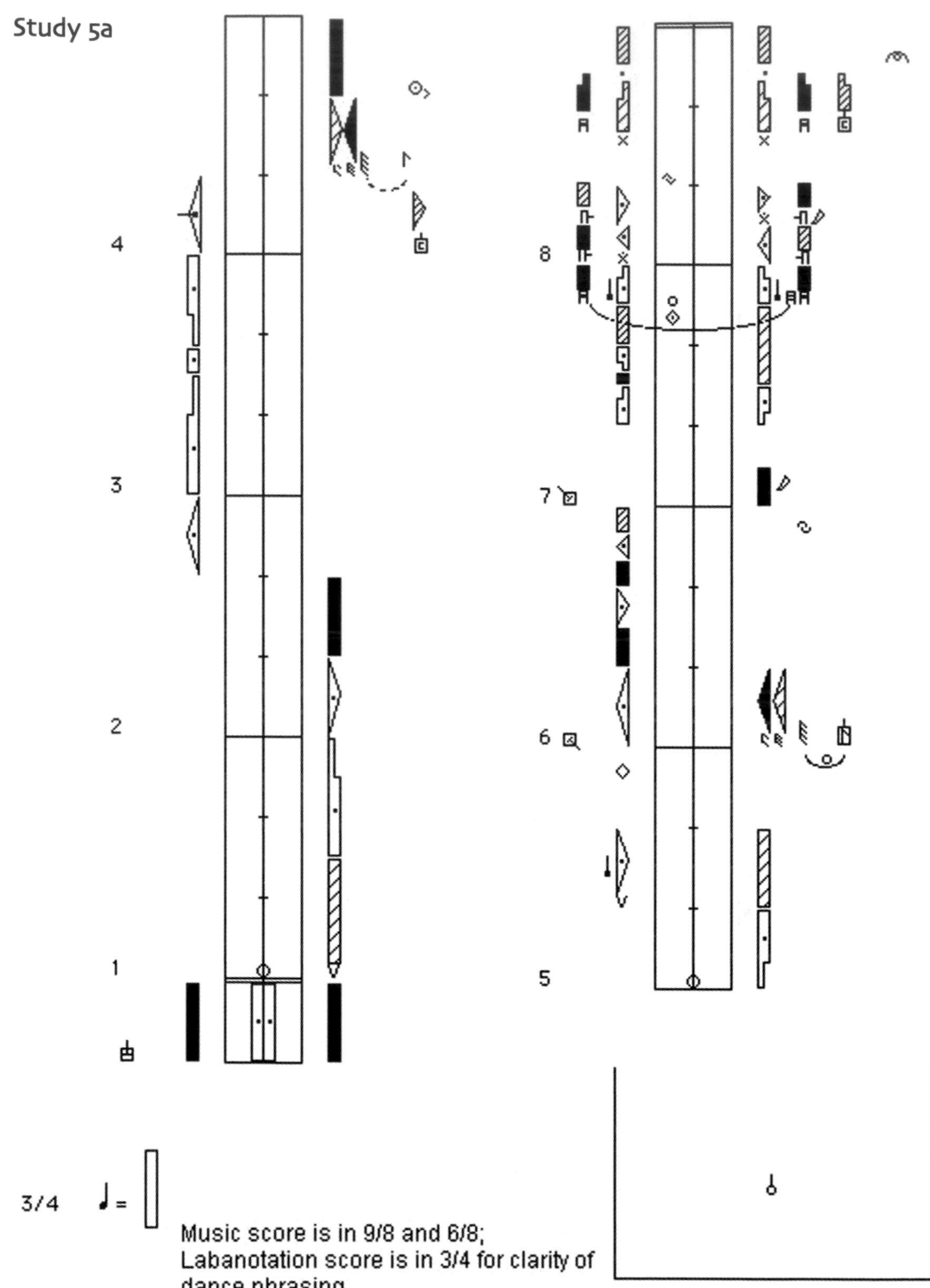

1
2
3
4
5
6
7
8
3/4
Music score is in 9/8 and 6/8;
Labanotation score is in 3/4 for clarity of
dance phrasing.

Study 5b

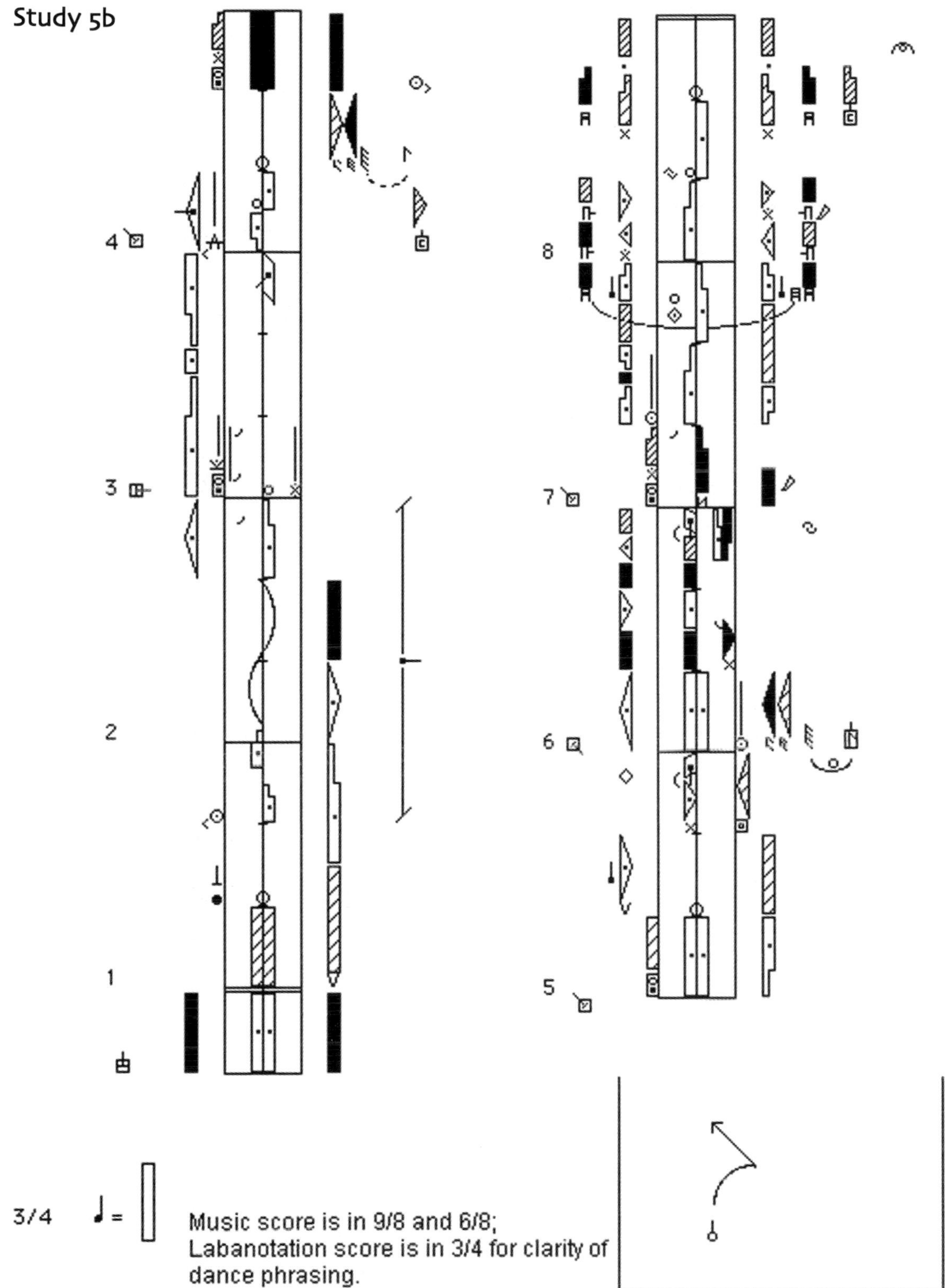
4
3
2
1
8
7
6
5
3/4
Music score is in 9/8 and 6/8;
Labanotation score is in 3/4 for clarity of dance phrasing.
1-8

5

Martin Blain

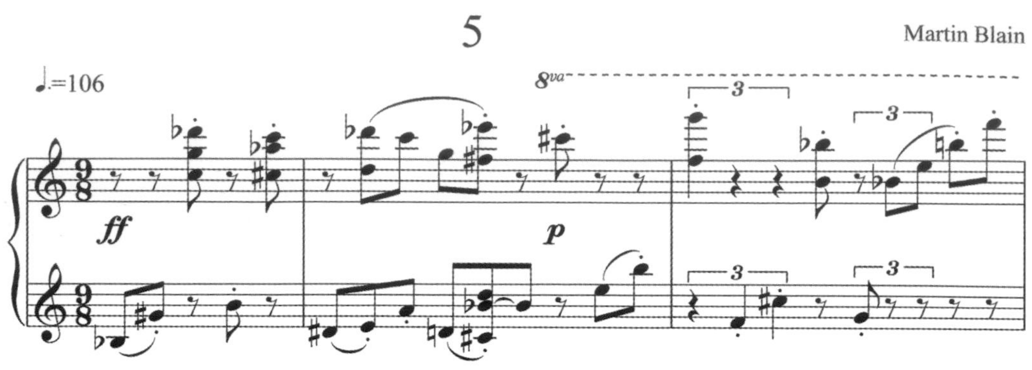

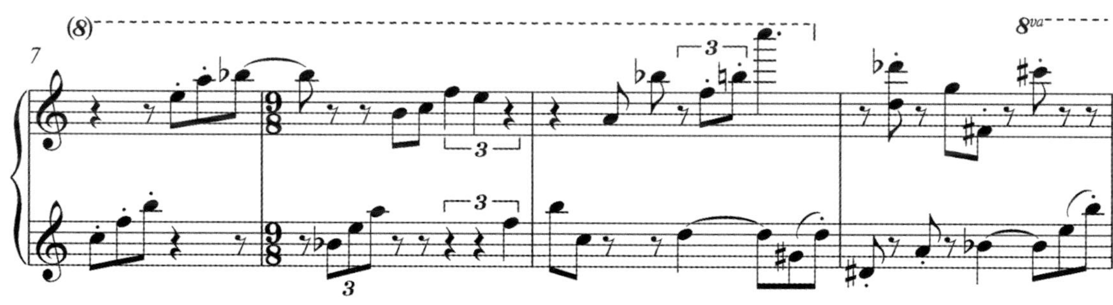

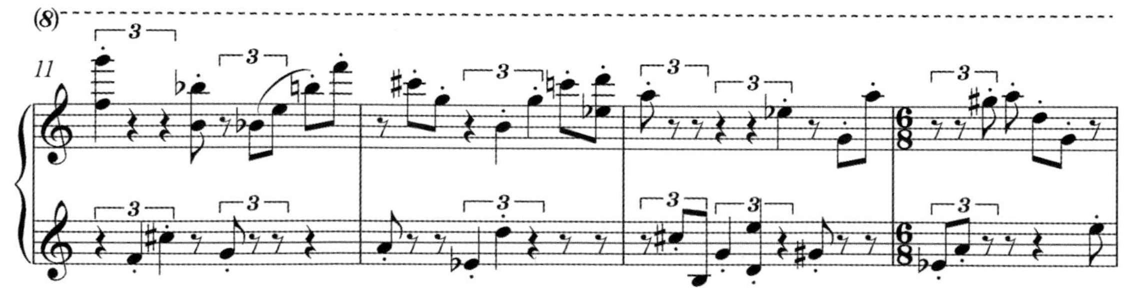

2

Other music suggestions

Title	Artist/composer	CD reference
Lyric waltz: Jazz Suite no. 2	Shostakovich	Decca 433 702-2
Chiquilin de Bachin	Piazzolla/Ferrer	EMI 5.6794432
The Swan: Carnival of the Animals	Saint-Saëns	Naxos 8.553039
Final Chorale: *St Matthew Passion*	J.S. Bach	Archiv 427 648-2
Gnarly Buttons 7. Stubble Crochet 10. Ständchen: The Little Serenade 13. Put your loving arms round me	John Adams	*John's Book of Alleged Dances.* Kronos Quartet Nonesuch 7559 79465 2
Broadcasting from Home 3. More Milk	Penguin Cafe Orchestra	Virgin EG Records EEGCD 38
Piano Works 15. 1ère Sarabande	Satie	Sony Essential Classics SBK 48 283

Study 6

This study is actually choreographed by Jennifer Jackson, rather than simply referring to her style. It may be performed as a solo (as in the plain version), or developed into canon form with several dancers (as in the complex version). Based in *danse d'école*, it employs recognisable features of ballet such as turn-out, extensions, *arabesques* and *developpés*. However, it also incorporates less familiar aspects such as rolling on the floor – a blatant contradiction of ballet's traditional defiance of gravity. Choreographers working in the ballet tradition during the last century have all explored ways of pushing the familiar vocabulary to be more or differently expressive – whether in the context of dramatic action, more abstract explorations of dance–music relationships, or through incorporating different dance styles, such as jazz.

The movement vocabulary is comparatively minimal, in the context of *danse d'école*, and thus the key factors to pay attention to are line, *épaulement*, the spatial relationship of dancers, and the relationship with the spaciousness of the music.

Other choreographers to experiment with:

— George Balanchine – extending and distorting 'classical' lines, incorporation of jazz elements (*Apollo*, *Agon*)
— William Forsythe – pushing the classical line to further extremes (*Steptext*)
— William Tuckett – perhaps involving some sense of character (*Duet for the Betterment of A*, *The Rime of the Ancient Mariner*)
— Jerome Robbins – again, developing a sense of character and situation, perhaps involving more jazz influences (*Fancy Free*, *Dances at a Gathering*)
— Mats Ek – incorporating characterisation, perhaps distorted body shapes, relationships (*Giselle*, *Swan Lake*, *Smoke*).

Further information on these choreographers is included at the end of this section.

Jennifer Jackson's choice of music for this study is *Chorale* for solo piano by Howard Skempton (in Howard Skempton, *Collected Piano Pieces*, Oxford University Press, 1996).

Study 6 plain: Notes

The starting position includes leg rotations, as this is a ballet study, but the degree of rotation is not the full 180° required of professional dancers! The relationship pins at the sides of the supports indicate the relationship of the feet to the centre line of the body, so one is directly in front of the other – fifth position.

The relationship pins for arm gestures bring the arms in front of the body rather than in a direct line with the shoulder, and the contraction pre-signs indicate the 'rounded' shape of many ballet arm positions.

In bar 4–5 the pivot in *arabesque* is shown through three separate pivoting movements on the supporting foot.

The final step forward leaves the left foot behind, toe in contact with the floor, in a conventional *dégagé derrière*, arms *bras bas.*

Study 6 (Jennifer Jackson): Notes

The key-sign at the bottom of the page indicates that the study is performed in full turn-out.

The relationship pins and one-degree contractions of many arm gestures, and the intermediate position of some arm gestures, are all commensurate with the *danse d'école* style.

The main new aspect is the long bracket running down the right-hand side of the staff. This shows that the study is performed in canon. The letters inside the bracket indicate when each dancer enters the canon. Each should enter with the beginning of the study, but a bar later than the dancer in front. The canon self-cancels, because the dancers exit at the end of the phrase (this is shown by the dotted line).

Intermediate positions, body key, parts of the foot, resultant touches, and supporting on different parts of the body are all included.

Bar 8 is the most complex in notation terms, but taken bit by bit it isn't really too bad. The kneeling position at the beginning is fairly normal – the inclusion of a pin inside the direction symbol alters the direction a little – a third towards diagonal back left, so crossing a little behind the body.

Sitting back on the left hip, the right foot is left flat on the floor in front (the leg is already bent from the previous movement).

The turn in the support column is joined to a new support symbol – the front of the torso – so this is the ending position: lying on the front. The arms are further contracted, and the contact bow swinging out from the palm signs indicate contact with the floor. The symbol above the knee symbols in the leg gesture column is a 'fold' of 2 degrees over the back surface.

The pivot continues and the support changes again to the hip. At the same time the torso begins to come upright – notice the intermediate direction: half-way between place high and forward high, only coming to full place high on the step up to standing.

Study 6: plain

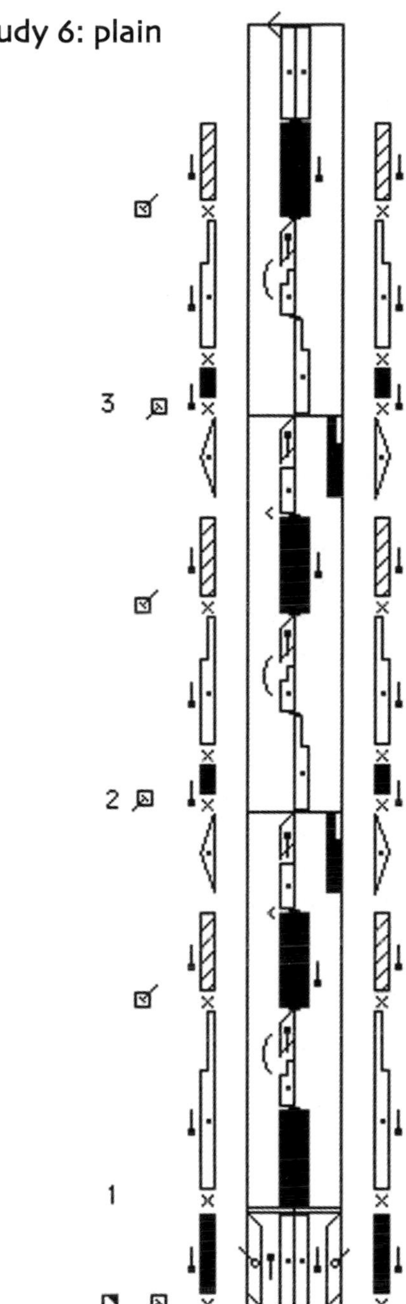

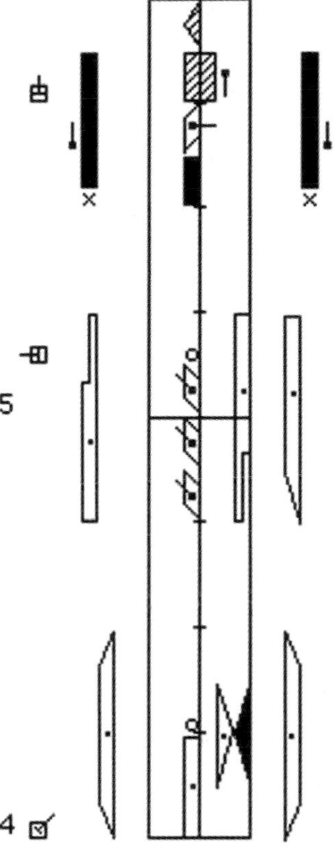

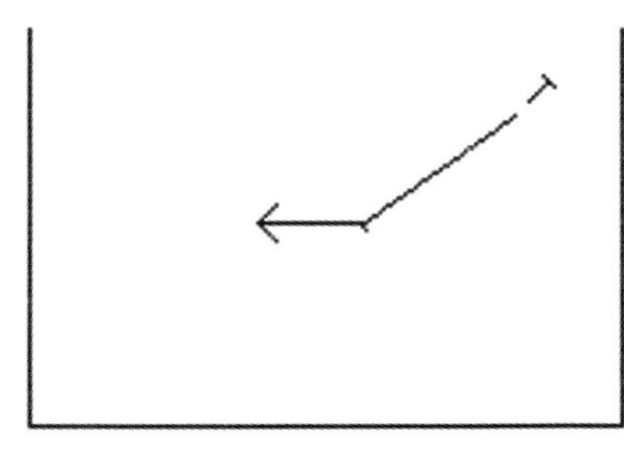

1-5

4/4 ♩ = ▯

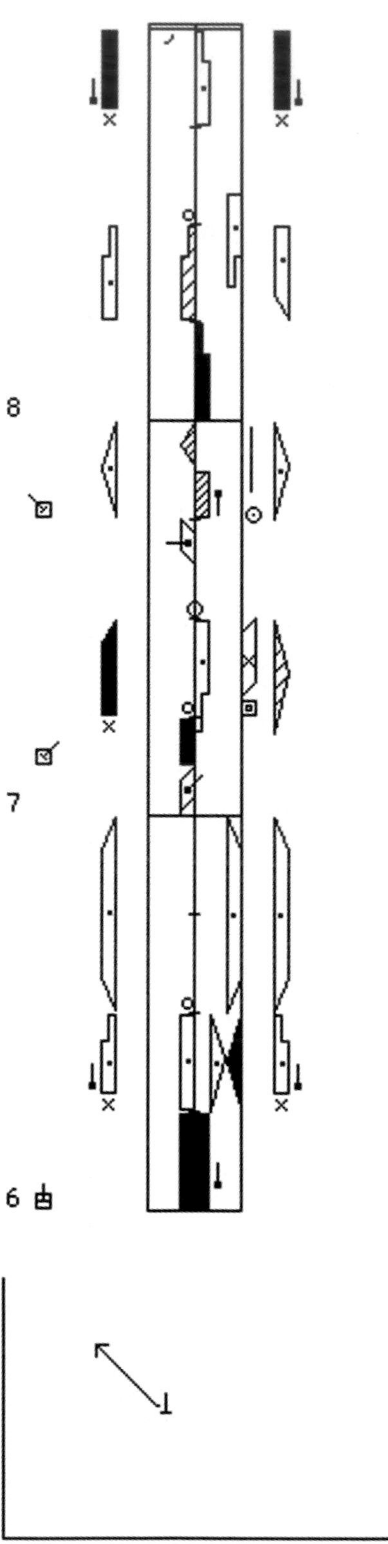

6-8

Study 6:
(Jennifer Jackson)

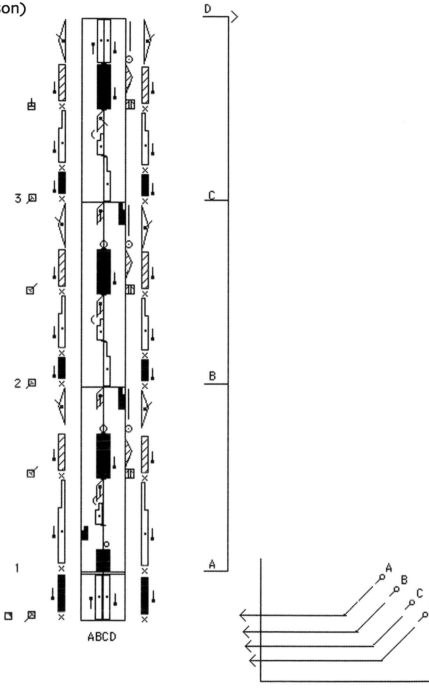

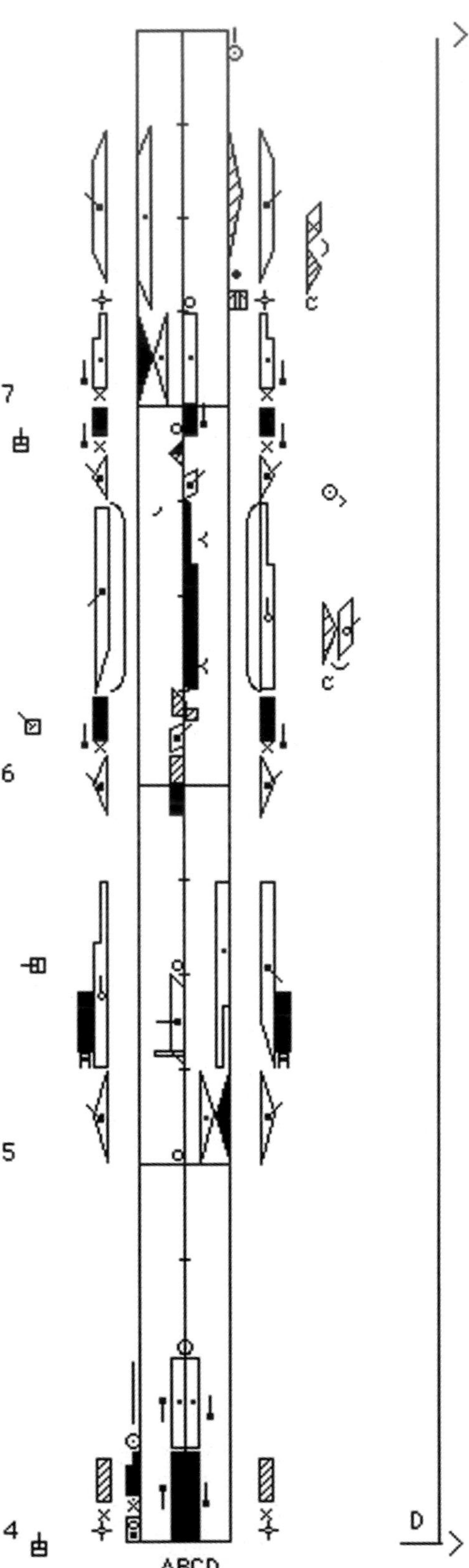
7
6
5
4
ABCD
D
C
C

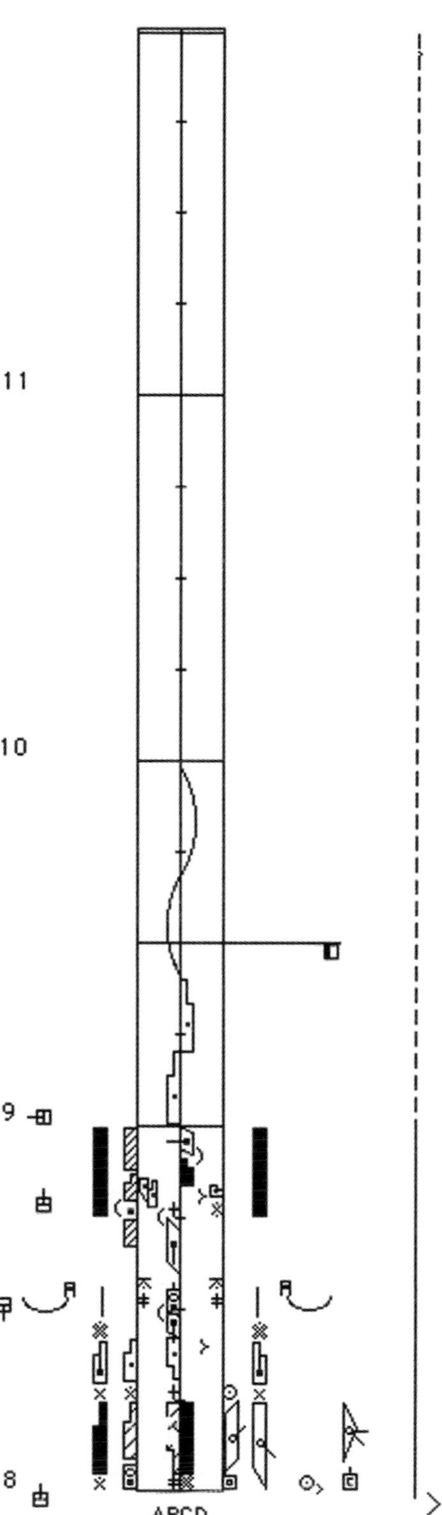
11
10
9
8
ABCD

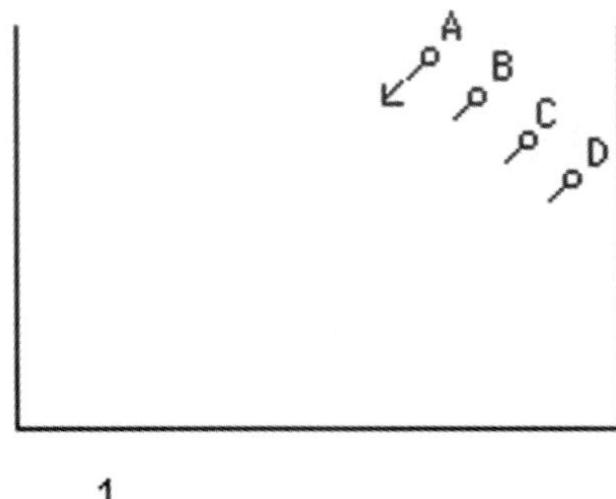

1

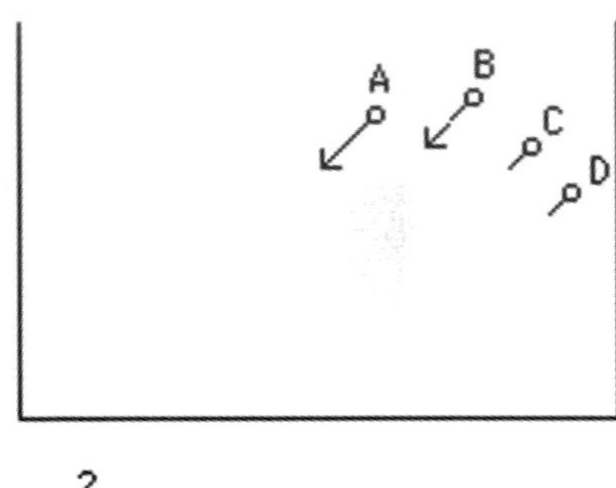

2

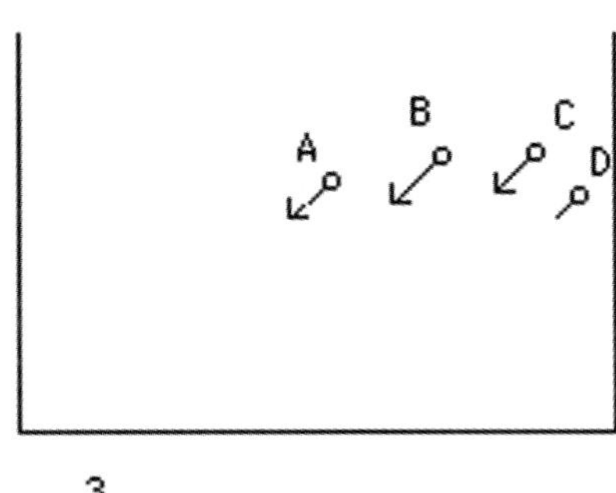

3

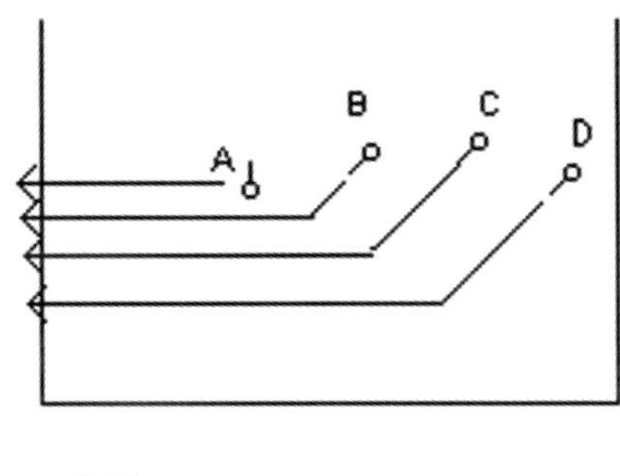

4-10

6

Martin Blain

Other music suggestions

Title	Artist/composer	CD reference
The barn owl has not flown away (On an overgrown path)	Janacek	Naxos 8.553586
Et la lune descend sur le temple qui fut	Debussy	Naxos 8.553292
Cantus in Memoriam Benjamin Britten	Arvo Pärt	Naxos 8.553750
The Odious	John Cage	*16 dances for soloist and company of 3* RCA 0902661574 2
Chorale	Howard Skempton	Sony SMK89617

References on choreographers cited

Richard Alston

Anderson, Z. (2005) 'DanceScene International: Richard Alston Dance Company', *The Dancing Times* April, p. 37.

Jordan, S. (1992) *Striding Out: Aspects of Contemporary and New Dance in Britain*, London, Dance Books Ltd.

Kane, A. (1998) 'Alston at 50: Still moving, still making giant strides', *The Dancing Times*, December, pp. 202–205.

Kane, A. (1999) 'Richard Alston' in Bremser, M. (ed.) *Fifty Contemporary Choreographers,* London and New York, Routledge.

Macaulay, A. (1998) 'Alston, Richard' in Cohen, S.-J. (ed.) *International Encyclopaedia of Dance, Vol. 1*, New York and Oxford, OUP.

Newman, B. (1987) 'Speaking of dance: Richard Alston', *The Dancing Times*, January, pp. 315–317.

Simpson, J. (2005) '*Seeing Hearing*: Richard Alston Dance Company by Jane Simpson', *Dance Now*, Summer 14/2, pp. 18–20.

George Balanchine

Carman, J. (2005) 'Teach-learn connection: Balanchine's teaching legacy', *Dance Magazine*, January, pp. 112–114.

Denby, E. (1987) 'Some thoughts about Classicalism and George Balanchine', *Dance Writing*, London, Dance Books, pp. 433–440.

Greskovic, R. (1993) 'Balanchine, George' in Bremser, M. (ed.) *International Dictionary of Ballet vol. 1: A–K* Detroit, St James Press.

Jordan, S. (2002) *Music Dances: Balanchine choreographs Stravinsky* (videocassette), New York, The George Balanchine Foundation.

Kai, U. (1998) 'Balanchine's way', *Ballet Review*, Winter 26/4, pp. 12–21.

Lee, C. (2000) 'George Balanchine and Neo-classicism' in *Ballet in Western Culture*, New York, Routledge.

Reynolds, N & M McCormick. (2003) *No Fixed Points: Dance in the Twentieth Century*, New Haven and London, Yale University Press.

Wilkins, D. (1996) 'Esthetic utilitarianism and the Balanchine style', *Ballet Review,* Fall 24/3, pp. 63–71.

Pina Bausch

Finkel, A. (1998) 'Bausch, Pina' in Cohen, S.-J. (ed.) *International Encyclopaedia of Dance, vol. 1,* New York and Oxford, OUP.

Gradinger, M. (1999) 'Pina Bausch' in Bremser, M. (ed.) *Fifty Contemporary Choreographers,* London and New York, Routledge.

Jays, D. (1999) 'Pina Bausch', *The Dancing Times,* March, pp. 523–525.

Kirchman, K. (1994) 'The totality of the body: An essay on Pina Bausch's aesthetic', *Ballett International,* May, pp. 37–43.

Nugent, A. (2003) 'Old Testament', *Dance Theatre Journal*, 19/1, pp. 22–24.

Kim Brandstrup

Burnside, F. (1994) 'Matthew Bourne and Kim Brandstrup: Telling other men's tales', *Dance Theatre Journal*, Spring/Summer 11/2, pp. 38–40.
Crabb, M. (2001) 'Kim Brandstrup's *Queen of Spades* for Les Grands Ballets Canadiens', *The Dancing Times*, December, pp. 17–19.
Pakes, A. (2003) 'A sense of anticipation: Choreographer Kim Brandstrup talks to Anna Pakes', *Dance Theatre Journal*, 19/1, pp. 8–11.
Walker, K, S. (1996) 'Arc Dance Company', *The Dancing Times*, April, pp. 667–669.
Walker, K, S. (2003) 'DanceScene International: Brandstrup's *Hamlet*', *Dancing Times*, June, p. 41.

Trisha Brown

Banes, S. (1987) *Terpsichore in sneakers. Post Modern Dance*, Hanover, Wesleyan University Press.
Banes, S. (1998) 'Brown, Trisha' in Cohen, S.-J. (ed.) *International Encyclopaedia of Dance, vol. 1*, New York and Oxford, OUP.
Dixon, M. (2002) 'The language of structure: Mike Dixon talks to Trisha Brown', *Dance Theatre Journal*, 18/4, pp. 16–19.
Goldberg, M. (1999) 'Trisha Brown' in Bremser, M. (ed.) *Fifty Contemporary Choreographers*, London and New York, Routledge.
Kraus, L. (2005) 'Trisha Brown: From the roofs of Soho to the Paris Opera Ballet – celebrating 35 years', *Dance Magazine*, April, pp. 32–36.
Reynolds, N. & McCormick, M. (2003) *No Fixed Points: Dance in the Twentieth Century*, New Haven and London, Yale University Press.
Roses-Thema, C. (1998) 'Brown, Trisha' in Benbow-Pfalzgraf, T. (ed.) *International Dictionary of Modern Dance,* Detroit, St James Press.

Jonathan Burrows

Anon. (2002) 'Playing the game harder: Jonathan Burrows in conversation', *Dance Theatre Journal*, 18/4, pp. 25–29.
Constanti, S. (1995/6) '*Blue Yellow*: Jonathan Burrow's new work for Sylvie Guillem', *Dance Theatre Journal*, Winter 12/3, pp. 4–5.
Duerden, R. (1999) 'Jonathan Burrows' in Bremser, M. (ed.) *Fifty Contemporary Choreographers*, London and New York, Routledge.
Duerden, R. (2001) 'Jonathan Burrows: Exploring the frontiers', *The Dancing Times*, March, pp. 551–557.
Jones, C. (1998) 'Burrows, Jonathan' in Benbow-Pfalzgraf, T. (ed.) *International Dictionary of Modern Dance*, Detroit, St James Press.

Rosemary Butcher

Elton, H. (2002) '*Water Works*: Rosemary Butcher Dance Company by Heather Elton', *Dance Now*, Autumn 11/3, pp. 93–95.
Jones, C. (1998) 'Butcher, Rosemary' in Benbow-Pfalzgraf, T. (ed.) *International Dictionary of Modern Dance*, Detroit, St James Press.

Jordan, S. (1986) 'Rosemary Butcher', *Dance Theatre Journal*, Summer 4/2, pp. 6–8.
Jordan, S. (1992) *Striding Out: Aspects of Contemporary and New Dance in Britain*, London, Dance Books.
Mackrell, J. (1992) *Out of Line: the Story of British New Dance*, London, Dance Books.
Sayers, L.-A. (1999) 'Rosemary Butcher' in Bremser, M. (ed.) *Fifty Contemporary Choreographers*, London and New York, Routledge.
Worth, L. (1999) 'Locating space: Dance and architecture in Rosemary Butcher's *3d*' in Adshead-Lansdale, J. (ed.) *Dancing Texts: Intertextuality in Interpretation*, London, Dance Books.

Lucinda Childs

Banes, S. (1987) *Terpsichore in Sneakers: Post Modern Dance*, Hanover, Wesleyan University Press.
Banes, S. (1998) 'Childs, Lucinda' in Cohen, S.-J. (ed.) *International Encyclopaedia of Dance, vol. 2*, New York and Oxford, OUP.
Burns, J. (1999) 'Lucinda Childs' in Bremser, M. (ed.) *Fifty Contemporary Choreographers*, London and New York, Routledge.
Marcotty, F. (1998) 'Childs, Lucinda' in Benbow-Pfalzgraf, T. (ed.) *International Dictionary of Modern Dance*, Detroit, St James Press.

Siobhan Davies

Jordan, S. (1992) *Striding Out: Aspects of Contemporary and New Dance in Britain*, London, Dance Books Ltd.
Jordan, S and B Rowell. (1998) 'Davis, Siobhan' in Cohen, S.-J. (ed.) *International Encyclopaedia of Dance, vol. 2*, New York and Oxford, OUP.
Jordan, S and S Whatley. (1999) 'Siobhan Davis' in Bremser, M. (ed.) *Fifty Contemporary Choreographers*, London and New York, Routledge.
Preston, S. (1999) 'Dance, music and literature: The construction and meanings through an interplay of texts in Siobhan Davies' *Bridge the Distance*' in Adshead-Lansdale, J. (ed.) *Dancing Texts: intertextuality in interpretation*, London, Dance Books.
Roy, S. (1998) 'Davies, Siobhan' in Benbow-Pfalzgraf, T. (ed.) *International Dictionary of Modern Dance*, Detroit, St James Press.
Roy, S. (2003) 'Profile: Siobhan Davies', *Dance Theatre Journal*, 19/3, pp. 11–15.
Whatley, S. (2002) 'Siobhan Davies' Plants *and Ghosts*', *The Dancing Times*, September, pp. 37–39.

Anne Teresa de Keersmaeker

Burt, R. (2004) 'Profile: Anne Teresa de Keersmaeker', *Dance Theatre Journal*, 19/4, pp. 36–39.
Felciano, R. (1998) 'de Keersmaeker, Anne Teresa' in Benbow-Pfalzgraf, T. (ed.) *International Dictionary of Modern Dance*, Detroit, St James Press.
Genter, S. (1999) 'Anna Teresa de Keersmaeker' in Bremser, M. (ed.) *Fifty Contemporary Choreographers*, London and New York, Routledge.
Jordan, S. (2003) '*Wedding Bouquet*: Anna Teresa de Keersmaeker and the tradition of *Les Noces* by Stephanie Jordan', *Dance Now*, Summer 12/2, pp. 73–78.
Mackrell, J. (2003) '*Rosas* – The Movie. Anna Teresa de Keersmaeker's *Counter Phrases* by Judith Mackrell', *Dance Now*, Summer 12/2, pp. 78–79.
Reynolds, N. & McCormick, M. (2003) *No Fixed Points: Dance in the Twentieth Century*, New Haven

and London, Yale University Press.

Mats Ek

Jennings, L. (2002) 'Good sex, bad sex: Preljocaj's *Le Sacre du Printemps* and Ek's *Carman* reviewed by Luke Jennings', *Dance Now*, Summer 11/2, pp. 17–20.
Nugent, A. (2001) 'Is Mats Ek a great choreographer?', *Dance Theatre Journal*, 17/3, pp. 32–35.
Poesio, G. (1999) 'Mats Ek' in Bremser, M. (ed.) *Fifty Contemporary Choreographers*, London and New York, Routledge.
Poesio, G. (2003) 'Choreographers Today – Mats Ek', *The Dancing Times*, October, pp. 22–25.
Stahle, A.G. (1998) 'Ek, Mats' in Cohen, S.-J. (ed.) *International Encyclopaedia of Dance, vol. 2*, New York and Oxford, OUP.

William Forsythe

Anthony, W. (1998) 'Forsythe in Milan & Frankfurt: Sand between the toes', *The Dancing Times*, December, pp. 247–249.
Genter, S. (1999) 'William Forsythe' in Bremser, M. (ed.) *Fifty Contemporary Choreographers*, London and New York, Routledge.
Gradinger, M. (1993) 'Forsythe, William' in Bremser, M. (ed.) *International Dictionary of Ballet, vol. 1: A–K*, Detroit, St James Press.
Jackson, J. (1999) 'Dancing Latin: William Forsythe's challenge to the balletic text' in Adshead-Lansdale, J. (ed.) *Dancing Texts: Intertextuality in Interpretation,* London, Dance Books.
Koegler, H. (1998)) 'Forsythe, William' in Cohen, S.-J. (ed.) *International Encyclopaedia of Dance, vol. 3*, New York and Oxford, OUP.
Nugent, A. (2003) 'Profile: William Forsythe', *Dance Theatre Journal*, 19/2, pp. 41–45.

David Gordon

Banes, S. (1987) *Terpsichore in Sneakers: Post Modern Dance*. Hanover, Wesleyan University Press.
Banes, S. (1998) 'Gordon, David' in Cohen, S.-J. (ed.) *International Encyclopaedia of Dance. vol. 3*, New York and Oxford, OUP.
Jordan, S. (1992) *Striding Out: Aspects of Contemporary and New Dance in Britain*, London, Dance Books.
Matheson, K. (1999) 'David Gordon' in Bremser, M. (ed.) *Fifty Contemporary Choreographers*, London and New York, Routledge.
Reynolds, N & McCormick, M. (2003) *No Fixed Points: Dance in the Twentieth Century*. New Haven and London, Yale University Press.

Jennifer Jackson

Macaulay, A. (1987) 'Bintley's Rossini, Jackson's Vivaldi', *The Dancing Times*, March, pp. 493–495.
Meisner, N. (1992) 'VoltAire: Lilian Baylis', *Dance and Dancers*, June, pp. 25–26.
Pitt, F. (1985) 'Royal Ballet at Covent Garden', *The Dancing Times*, September, pp. 1033–1035.

Shobana Jeyasingh

Hale, C. (2003) 'Peripheral vision: Catherine Hale explores Shobana Jeyasingh's *(h)interland*', *Dance Theatre Journal*, 19/1, pp. 41–45.

Jeyasingh, S. (1997) 'Text Context Dance', *Choreography and Dance*, 4/2, pp. 31–34.
Jeyasingh, S. (1998) 'Imaginary homelands: Creating a new dance language' in Carter, A. (ed.) *The Routledge Dance Studies Reader*, London, Routledge.
Roy, S. (1998) 'Jeyasingh, Shobana' in Benbow-Pfalzgraf, T. (ed.) *International Dictionary of Modern Dance*, Detroit, St James Press.
Sanders, L. (2001) 'Choreographers Today – Shobana Jeyasingh', *The Dancing Times*, September, pp. 1077–1083.

Akram Khan
Anderson, Z. (2000) 'Dance scene, new moves: Akram Khan/Dansgroep Krisztina de Chtel', *The Dancing Times*, May, pp. 728–729.
Anderson, Z. (2005) 'DanceScene International: Akram Khan Company's *Ma*', *The Dancing Times*, February, pp. 49–50.
Kent, S. (2002) 'If only but also: Akram Khan's *Kaash* by Sarah Kent', *Dance Now*, Autumn 11/3, pp. 71–73.
Vasudevan, P. (2002) 'Clarity within chaos: Akram Khan talks to Preeti Vasudevan about the classical, the contemporary and creating *Kaash*', *Dance Theatre Journal*, 18/1, pp. 16–19.
Willis, M. (2001) 'Dancer Profile: Akram Khan', *The Dancing Times*, March, p. 588.

Jiri Kylian
Kloos, H. (1993) 'Kylian, Jiri' in Bremser, M. (ed.) *International Dictionary of Ballet, vol 1, A–K*, Detroit, St James Press.
Reynolds, N & McCormick, M. (2003) *No Fixed Points: Dance in the Twentieth Century*, New Haven and London, Yale University Press.
Sayers, L-A. (1999) 'Jiri Kylian' in Bremser, M. (ed.) *Fifty Contemporary Choreographers*, London and New York, Routledge.
Utrecht, L. (1998) 'Kylian, Jiri' in Cohen, S.-J. (ed.) *International Encyclopaedia of Dance, vol. 4*, New York and Oxford, OUP.

Wayne McGregor
Anderson, Z. (2002) 'DanceScene International: Rambert Dance Company', *The Dancing Times*, November, pp. 63–65.
Boxberger, E. (1997) 'The millennarium: Wayne McGregor in London', *Ballett International*, December, p. 56.
Hansen, S. (2001) 'Choreographers Today – Wayne McGregor, twenty-first century choreographers', *The Dancing Times*, June, pp. 799–801.
Jays, D. (2002) 'DanceScene International: Random Dance and others in London', *The Dancing Times*, April, pp. 61–63.

Kenneth Macmillan
Anderson, K. (2005) 'Macmillan at work', *The Dancing Times*, March, pp. 15–17.
Mackrell, J. (1997) *Reading Dance*, London, Penguin Group.
Reynolds, N & McCormick, M. (2003) *No Fixed Points: Dance in the Twentieth Century*, New Haven and London, Yale University Press.

Seymour, L. (2002) 'Kenneth Macmillan – The Early Years', *The Dancing Times*, March, pp. 23–31.
Thorpe, E. (1993) 'Kenneth Macmillan' in Bremser, M. (ed.) *International Dictionary of Ballet, vol. 2 L–Z*, Detroit, St James Press.
Thorpe, E. (1985) *Kenneth Macmillan – the man and his ballets*, London, Hamish Hamilton.

Mark Morris
Acocella, J. (1998) 'Morris, Mark' in Cohen, S.-J. (ed.) *International Encyclopaedia of Dance, vol. 4*, New York and Oxford, OUP.
Acocella, J. (1999) 'Mark Morris' in Bremser, M. (ed.) *Fifty Contemporary Choreographers*, London and New York, Routledge.
Anderson, Z. (1994) 'Mark Morris Dance Group', *The Dancing Times*, October, p. 38.
Bannerman, H. (2002) 'Profile: Mark Morris', *Dance Theatre Journal*, 18/4, pp. 34–36.
Clarke, M. (1999) 'Mark Morris', *The Dancing Times*, November, p. 107.
Macaulay, A. (1994) '*L'Allegro, il Penseroso, ed il Moderato*', *The Dancing Times,* August, pp. 1091–1093.
Reynolds, N & McCormick, M. (2003) *No Fixed Points: Dance in the Twentieth Century*, New Haven and London, Yale University Press.

Lloyd Newson
Anon. (1990) 'DV8 Physical Theatre in Rouen', *Dance Theatre Journal*, Late Summer 8/2, pp. 4–5.
Leask, J. (1999) 'Lloyd Newson' in Bremser, M. (ed.) *Fifty Contemporary Choreographers*, London and New York, Routledge.
Hutera, D. (1998) 'Newson, Lloyd' in Benbow-Pfalzgraf, T. (ed.) *International Dictionary of Modern Dance*, Detroit, St James Press.
Meisner, N. (1990) '*You Must Go On*: Nadine Meisner considers DV8's latest work and talks to its choreographer Lloyd Newson', *Dance and Dancers*, October, pp. 18–19.
Prickett, S. (2003) 'Profile: Lloyd Newson', *Dance Theatre Journal*, 19/1, pp. 27–31.

Angelin Preljocaj
Jennings, L. (2002) 'Good sex, bad sex: Preljocaj's *Le Sacre du Printemps* and Ek's *Carman* reviewed by Luke Jennings', *Dance Now*, Summer 11/2, pp. 17–20.
Mathieu, M. (1998) 'Angelin Preljocaj', in Benbow-Pfalzgraf, T. (ed.) *International Dictionary of Modern Dance*, Detroit, St James Press.
Nugetn, A. (1993/4) 'Through a wide-angled lens', *Dance Now*, Winter 2/4, pp. 22–7.
Reynolds, N & McCormick, M. (2003) *No Fixed Points: Dance in the Twentieth Century*, New Haven and London, Yale University Press.
Wagner-Bergelt, B. (1996) 'The classical choreographer between abstraction and expression', *Ballett International–Tanz Aktuel*, April, pp. 34–37.

Yvonne Rainer
Banes, S. (1987) *Terpsichore in Sneakers: Post Modern Dance*, Hanover, Wesleyan University Press.
Banes, S. (1998) 'Rainer, Yvonne' in Cohen, S.-J. (ed.) *International Encyclopaedia of Dance, vol. 5*, New York and Oxford, OUP.
Raugust, K. (1998) 'Rainer, Yvonne' in Benbow-Pfalzgraf, T. (ed.) *International Dictionary of Modern*

Dance, Detroit, St James Press.
Reynolds, N & McCormick, M. (2003) *No Fixed Points: Dance in the Twentieth Century*, New Haven and London, Yale University Press.

Jerome Robbins

Goldner, N. (2002) 'Round Robbins: Jerome Robbins' *Fancy Free* by Nancy Goldner', *Dance Now*, Autumn 1/3, pp. 42–47.
Greg , L. (2001) *Dance With Demons: The Life of Jerome Robbins*, New York, G.P. Putnam's Sons.
Hering, D. (1993) 'Robbins, Jerome' in Bremser, M. (ed.) *International Dictionary of Ballet, vol. 2 L–Z*, Detroit, St James Press.
McDonagh, M. (2002) 'Round Robbins: Jerome Robbins on DVD by Maitland McDonagh', *Dance Now*, Autumn 11/3, pp. 47–51.
Pitt, F. (1999) 'Jerome Robbins and other dances in Paris', *The Dancing Times*, May, pp. 747–751.
Reynolds, N & McCormick, M. (2003) *No Fixed Points: Dance in the Twentieth Century*, New Haven and London, Yale University Press.
Schlundt, C, L. (1989) *Dance in the Musical Theatre: a guide: Jerome Robbins and his peers, 1934 – 1965*, London and New York, Garland.

Yolande Snaith

Duerden, R. (2002) 'Yolande Snaith: Creating her own reality', *The Dancing Times*, January, pp. 33–39.
Henshaw, D. (1990) 'Yolande Snaith', *Dance Theatre Journal*, Autumn 8/3, p. 26.
Hunt, M. (1990) 'Reviews…international', *Dance Magazine*, February, pp. 108–109.
Phillips, A. (1992) 'Review: Dance Quorum's *No Respite*, Dance Umbrella at the Place, October 1991', *Dance Theatre Journal*, Spring 9/3, pp. 36–37.
Rubidge, S. (1988) 'Steps in time. A television director's perspective by Sarah Rubidge', *Dance Theatre Journal*, Summer 6/1, pp. 15 17.
Sayers, L-A. (1988) 'Spring Loaded. The Place Theatre, March/April 1998', *Dance Theatre Journal*, Autumn 6/2, pp. 10–11.
Sayers, L A. (1989) 'Off the Euston Road: Lesley-Ann Sayers selects five companies for discussion from the Spring Loaded and April in Paris seasons', *Dance Theatre Journal*, Autumn 7/2, pp. 32–35.

Paul Taylor

Burns, J F. (1993) 'Taylor, Paul' in Bremser, M. (ed.) *International Dictionary of Ballet, vol. 2 L–Z*. Detroit, St James Press.
Kane, A. (1998) 'Taylor, Paul' in Cohen, S.J. (ed.) *International Encyclopaedia of Dance, vol. 6*, Oxford and New York, OUP.
Kane, A. (1999) 'Paul Taylor' in Bremser, M. (ed.) *Fifty Contemporary Choreographers*, London and New York, Routledge.
Reynolds, N & McCormick, M. (2003) *No Fixed Points: Dance in the Twentieth Century*, New Haven and London, Yale University Press.
Ulrich, A. (2005) 'Paul Taylor's 50th Anniversary: Roundtable of dancers past and present', *Dance Magazine*, March, pp. 32–35.

Twyla Tharp

Couch, N. (1998) 'Tharp, Twyla' in Benbow-Pfalzgraf, T. (ed.) *International Dictionary of Modern Dance*, Detroit, St James Press.

Craine, D. (2003) 'Mind Games: Twyla Tharp talks to Debra Craine', *Dance Now*, Summer 12/2, pp. 51–56.

Gradinger, M,. (1994) 'An American evening', *Ballett International*, July, pp. 8–9.

Harris, D. (1999) 'Twyla Tharp' in Bremser, M. (ed.) *Fifty Contemporary Choreographers*, London and New York, Routledge.

Macaulay, A. (1998) 'Thoroughly Modern Twyla', *The Dancing Times*, October, pp. 41–43.

Newman, B, (1994) 'American visit: Cunningham in New York, Tharp in Washington', *The Dancing Times*, December, pp. 243–245.

Reynolds, N & McCormick, M. (2003) *No Fixed Points: Dance in the Twentieth Century*, New Haven and London, Yale University Press.

Shapiro, L. (1998) 'Tharp, Twyla' in Cohen, S. (ed.) *International Encyclopaedia of Dance, vol. 6*, Oxford and New York, OUP.

William Tuckett

Anderson, Z. (1999) 'Royal Ballet Dance Bites', *The Dancing Times*, April, pp. 643–645.

Gilbert, J. (2004) 'Go to Hell: William Tuckett's *The Soldier's Tale* by Jenny Gilbert', *Dance Now*, Autumn 13/3, pp. 103–105.

Jays, D. (1995) 'Dance Bites', *The Dancing Times*, March, pp. 583–585.

Robertson, A. (2000) 'William Tuckett', *Dance Now*, Summer 9/3, pp. 86–87.

Part 2: Philosophical Issues

2.1: Critical essays

2.1.1: Choreographic style – choreographic intention and embodied ideas

Bonnie Rowell

Introduction to choreographic style – and what it's not

This may seem a strange place to begin, but, setting aside the question of what choreographic style analysis might entail for the time being, there are some procedures that may be identified straight away in terms of *what it's not*, and these might point us in the right direction for where to start the discussion. What choreographic style is most definitely *not*, then, is a form of choreographic caricature, by which I mean a hotchpotch of signature moves and features that have been identified and then re-assembled *without reference or recourse to intention or meaning* – a sort of 'choreography by numbers'. Choreography and, by extension, the study of choreographic style, has to make sense. It embodies ideas that are accessible to others – indeed, 'making sense' and the embodiment of ideas are crucial issues here. But to whom do the ideas belong (choreographer, dancer and/or viewer?) and how do we access them? This paper begins with an examination of prevailing accounts of choreographic style to help to tease out the problem further. It will then discuss ways in which accounts of embodiment theory can facilitate our critical understanding of dances, and ideas about the kinds of dance *knowledge* that are required to access them. Lastly, it will test these ideas briefly against some practical examples.

Two accounts of choreographic style

With the proliferation of dance degree programmes throughout the UK, students have become increasingly sophisticated in their movement observations and style analyses. This is in no small part due to pioneering work in dance analysis carried out by Janet Adshead-Lansdale and her team during the 1980s and 1990s, which laid the foundations for systematic and structured response to dance works. The model for dance analysis that emerged then also placed an emphasis on dance meaning and interpretation – an important move, because it focused on an account of dance as primarily meaning-bearing. This was by no means a given at that time.

So, the traditional 'dance analysis' answer to the question 'What is choreographic style?' goes something like the following: 'the typical selection of materials by a choreographer, with regard to movement vocabulary, dynamic range, use of space, structuring devices and so on, in relation to thematic material' (after Adshead 1988). This model is still widely employed, even though she herself and her team members have moved on in their approach. Another, equally well-respected model by Susan Foster (1986) further democratises the process by paying respect to the choreographer's (and dancers') working practice. For example, Trisha Brown's task-based choreography, one could argue, demands an intellectual response from the dancers, together with their creative engagement; Merce Cunningham's stylistic precedent requires individuality and esoteric bodily articulation from his dancers; while Pina Bausch and DV8's workshop-based choreographic practice implicates the dancer as a person with emotional history and so on. All these processes can be seen clearly to have some bearing on the choreographic statement. Thus the choreographer's attitude to the dancers and dancers' representation of self within the dance (and knowledge of these) become key issues in determining how we perceive the dances, and hence how we understand them. This constitutes a shift away from an emphasis on the dance as *object* of understanding, towards a more contextually based model. A further shift occurs when the viewer's agency is acknowledged, in line with issues raised by post-structuralism (Foster 1986; Adshead-Lansdale 1999). So the process of analysis then becomes interactive, with the viewer privileged as responsible for the construction of meaning.

But there are problems embedded within these approaches at a very basic level and which, to be fair, both authors acknowledge. First, the account of choreographic style as the choreographer's 'selection of materials' views the dance in terms of its perceptible features. Any concerns with what the choreographer *intended* the dance to be about are seen as irrelevant – and rightly so – because the choreographer's intentions can only be apparent within the (material) choreography. If they are not, then the choreographer has simply failed to communicate ideas adequately. But clearly that cannot be the end of the matter, because we draw on contextual knowledge[4] all the time in our understanding of dances. The relationship then between dance 'text' and its context needs more detailed examination.

Furthermore, questions that are relevant to dance appreciation as well as to choreographic invention, such as 'What do we see?' and 'How does it make us feel?', assume a connection between dance features and their reception that is not at all obvious when the viewer's position remains inadequately acknowledged, and this in turn invokes difficult questions to do with the nature of perception. Tensions, then, between the two general positions are still very much in evidence (irrespective of Adshead's and Foster's current positions), but I would like to sow the seed here of another line through, drawing on my own research, in looking at the problem in a different way (Rowell 2003).

Choreographic intention

While the choreographer's psychological state cannot or should not be mistaken for the dance itself, nevertheless it does indeed impinge upon the way in which the dance is viewed and understood. One example from literature, which is often used to illustrate the point, is Jonathan Swift's *A Modest Proposal* (1729), in which Swift puts forward a solution to both the Irish

[4] The Adshead *et al* model acknowledges the role of context, of course, urging us to read dance components in relation to their character and qualities in order to access meaning. The point remains however, that in this model it is the dance's materiality that is privileged.

potato famine and the population explosion: breed babies for the dinner table! To interpret this work literally, as a serious proposition to indulge in cannibalism for social ends, would be to misunderstand the work[5]; and we know, from Swift's other writing amongst other things, that we *should* read it as satire. We could say that Swift *intended* the piece to be read as satire, and in this sense the author's intention directs us to an appropriate way of reading the work. It is debatable whether we would be directed to an appropriate way of reading from the text alone – that is, looking only at perceptible features as 'evidence'.

Swift's is an extreme example of something that usually happens far less obviously, and Mark Morris's 1982 dance, *Songs that tell a story*, provides an example that is closer to home. In the 'Robe of White' section, Morris choreographs to a Country and Western song by the Louvin Brothers. This tells the story of a mother waiting anxiously for the postman's knock for news of her soldier-son; the long awaited letter instead relates his death. The song bears the heavy sentimentality associated with the Country and Western genre, and the three dancers act out the words of the song in an almost literal way, employing mime and melodramatic gesture and invoking a number of diverse dance conventions, including those embedded within the dramatic emotionalism of Martha Graham's technique. At one point, Morris himself performs a deep contraction accompanied by a yearning gesture, which has become a hallmark of Graham's movement vocabulary. And yet Morris is neither proposing a dance drama nor poking fun at the genre, even though both these possibilities are on the surface, hinted at, if we look at the 'internal' evidence alone.

The issue hinges on how it is possible to know this from the perceptible features of the dance work: how I know that an interpretation that takes the work literally, as a 'send up' say, of Country and Western music, taking in Graham's choreography along the way, is an incorrect interpretation, and one that misses the point. I know this because I have seen other works by Morris and know him to be a complex and sincere choreographer: to have a tendency to ironic humour and not only be renowned for his musicality, but also have musically diverse interests. These last two points would lead me to believe, at the very least, that he takes the relationship between music and dance seriously, whatever the music's origin. These considerations lead towards a more generous understanding of Morris's acknowledgement of, and sympathy for, the place of popular culture in ordinary people's emotional lives, whereas just considering the perceptible features of the dance might lead to misunderstanding, as we have seen. But thinking about the context of Morris's work shows us that it *is* misunderstanding, and leads us towards a more appropriate understanding. If this is regarded as looking at Morris's *intention*, then it is far removed from looking into Morris's *mind*, or indeed asking the choreographer what he meant, just as it is with the Swift example. The choreographer's working process, his attitude towards the dancers and the dancers' expression of self within the dance, can similarly be seen

[5] McFee argues that perception is concept-mediated, and consequently we need to correctly identify and draw upon appropriate concepts in order to understand dance works. For a full examination of the dangers of misperceiving a dance work, see McFee 1992, pp. 42–44.

as contextual knowledge all of which contributes towards appropriate explanations of the dance.

If we now turn to the second (arguably poststructuralist) account of choreographic style, that of the reader as instrumental in the construction of meaning, then we see that the problems here are to do with boundaries: the possible letting-in of rampant subjectivism, together with the loss of distinctive criteria by which to judge an artwork. If I as the reader am active in constructing meaning, how do I test whether my observations are relevant to an appreciation of the dance, or merely subject to individual whim (such as disliking the dance because I associate it with the headache I had when I went to see it) or even whether my observations are correct?

Both these positions depend upon misunderstandings in the relationship between text and context: with the former position (the one that deals only in material, perceptible features) identifying distinctions that are over-simplistic and unsustainable, and the latter position (the one that privileges the viewer in the construction of meaning) conflating the two to a degree that may be unacceptable.

Cavell, materials and ideas

The philosopher Stanley Cavell's discussion of materials and medium can be put to use here. In his discussion, Cavell (1969) focuses on the nature of the work of art itself, as a *meaning-bearing* object: that is, an object in which the makers' *ideas* are *embodied*. He says that in looking for an answer to the question 'Why this?' within an artwork (what is the significance of this particular selection of material features or components?) we are not being asked to look *outside* the work at extraneous 'facts', but rather 'further *into* the work'. In other words, contextual information in all its manifestations is very much a *part* of the work, and not external to it. Cavell begins with an examination of the concept of 'medium' and takes issue with some common philosophical assumptions:

> Philosophers will sometimes say that sound is the medium of music, paint of painting, wood and stone of sculpture, words of literature ... What needs recognition is that wood or stone would not be a medium of sculpture *in the absence of the art of sculpture* ... The idea of a medium is not simply that of a physical material, but of a material-in-certain-characteristic-applications. (Cavell 1969, p. 221)

Cavell draws our attention to the problem that, in speaking of art objects as *objects*, we talk of their organisation, but that tells us nothing about *why* the object is as it is, nor *how* it means what it does. In Cavell's terms, artworks are characteristically human actions, and in order to have insight into 'why this and not this?' we must look into the intentions inherent in the actions, not in terms of 'some internal, prior mental event causally connected with outward effects' (Cavell 1969, p. 226), but in terms of seeking explanations for human actions – 'discovering an intention is a way of discovering an explanation' (Cavell 1969, p. 235).

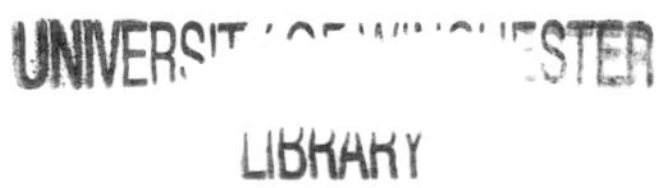

> Intention is no more an efficient cause of an object of art than it is of a human action; in both cases it is a way of understanding the thing done, of describing what happens. (Cavell 1969, p. 230)

Intention then, in Cavell's sense and in the sense outlined above, both acknowledges the materiality of the artwork and connects the physical object with the ideas that it manifests. So, if we follow Cavell's thought, here is a consideration of choreographic style in terms of human actions, and an account of choreographic analysis in terms of accessing and understanding the ideas that are embodied within dances. In doing this, we acknowledge the agency of the choreographer – and contextual information thereby becomes a part of the dance – as well as the agency of the viewer in terms of bringing the appropriate conceptual framework to bear.

If we tease this out in relation to the previous dance example, returning to Morris's *Songs that tell a story,* it becomes clear that information (say, from knowledge of the choreographer's other works) may direct us towards appreciating the ironic tone and hence to appropriate ways of interpreting the dance. This might still lead us to see, for example, Morris's contraction and over-blown gesture as camp, but camp with affectionate overtones – in the full knowledge of Morris's deep understanding of, and empathy with, the human predicament – which we know from a knowledge of his works, life and general world outlook. It is important to make the point that this does not necessarily lead to a single unitary way of interpreting the dance. Furthermore, the case will be subject to debate in line with arguments concerning, for example, *which* of Morris's other dances are the most relevant works to compare with *Songs.*

In accepting Cavell's definition of artistic medium as 'materials-in-certain-characteristic applications', then, an account of dance has also to include the employment and deployment of the dancers in certain ways that are characteristic of a particular choreographer and such that they (the dancers in relation to the other components) embody her/his intentions. This constitutes a shift away from the materiality of dances towards a concept of dances as *embodied ideas*. The choreographer and dancers contribute towards the ideas, but perhaps in most instances the choreographer retains the position of prime mover and has the final say, as artistic director commanding an overview of the choreographic statement. But an account of dance as 'embodied ideas' also has to acknowledge the active role of the viewer, because it involves reciprocity and so perception is identified as creative.

A reciprocal relationship: perception as creative and interactive

The notion of a reciprocal relationship between artwork – or, in our case, dance – and audience is important to us on two counts. First, it further fleshes out the idea of an artwork, not as an object, but as a medium for human action and intention. Second, it offers an adequate account of the role of the viewer and thus permits a check against at least some of the dangers of an 'anything goes' ethos that may be embedded within a post-structuralist approach. The art historian and philosopher Paul Crowther argues the case of perception as a reciprocal activity. Implicit within his argument is a further important point: that artworks are inherently understandable and valuable. Crowther (1993) puts forward what he calls an 'ecological' thesis concerning artistic appreciation and critical analysis[6]. He argues that artworks are the complex entities that we make, that both reflect and give sense to the world. As such, they are an important means by which we understand our interaction with others and with 'otherness'. But art is appreciated, at least to some extent, in its objects; that is, artworks have both physical and conceptual dimensions and they thus serve to ground our experience in all its richness, without losing the sense of unity of that experience. So the appreciation of artworks is a process that is in contradistinction to analysing our experience alone. Crowther gives the example of philosophical thought here, in which we fragment that experience and can never fully grasp the total nature of our inherence in the world. Artworks (dances) therefore fulfil very important functions within our lives in unifying our experience of the world: in re-unifying our physical and sensory experience.

The relationship between self and other is therefore reciprocal, in that we too are changed as a result of our interaction with the world (and especially our interaction with artworks) – so that we are constantly repositioning ourselves in relation to the world. From this, we can see that at least some of the problems to do with our appreciation of artworks under the conditions of postmodernity (and post-structuralism) are provided with solutions; in the re-positioning of the subject, this account of embodiment offers a position of stability within an unstable postmodern world, and problems to do with indeterminacy, arbitrariness and subjectivism are thereby tackled. An important correlate of this is that coherence and decipherability are acknowledged as inherent values of artworks.

When we apply all this to the special case of dance in which the physicality of the medium embodies a separate set (separate from the choreographer) of human intentions, then we see that the relationship between choreographer, dancer and audience is very specifically highlighted – all as interacting and intentional, embodied entities.

To summarise the position so far: we have learnt that dances are human actions (by choreographer and dancers); so in order to understand them, we must look into the intentions inherent in their actions. Within dances, the choreographer's intentions or ideas are embodied by the dancers and embedded within the other components. This account also acknowledges the active role of the viewer, because there is a reciprocal relationship between viewer and artwork, and in this way perception is identified as creative and imaginative. This account of reciprocity in the perceptual process may have important implications for notation, but that is a matter to be explored elsewhere.

At a basic level, this process invokes an account of choreographic style that starts with what you see and hear, and goes on to explain 'why' and 'how' what you see and hear are as they are. These questions involve acknowledgement and understanding of the choreographer's conceptual framework, as well as the creative and imaginative engagement of the viewer.

[6] Crowther's thesis draws on ideas from Kant and Merleau Ponty, and in so doing provides a pluralist perspective that seeks to unite traditional Western analytic and continental philosophical positions.

Analysis of choreographic style – 'noticing' and knowledge

So we turn now to an examination of the notion of the choreographer's conceptual framework and to questions about how to access it: how to know what to notice. From Cavell, we have learnt that, in looking for an answer to the question 'Why this?' within an artwork, we are not being asked to look *outside* the work at extraneous knowledge, but rather 'further *into* the work'. In other words, contextual information in all its manifestations is very much a *part* of the work, rather than something you find out about, although 'finding out about' forms a part of the process. It is not, however, an end in itself, and all the research in the world is not going to illuminate a dance when the viewer does not possess the necessary perceptual 'fitness'.

This still, however, begs the question of how we *know* what to notice, what to attend to. Here I draw upon Graham McFee's model of perception of artworks as a 'species of noticing' (2004). McFee argues that *artistic knowledge* is central to understanding dance, and he makes an important distinction here between *knowledge that is manifest in art*, in contrast to knowledge *about* art (McFee 2004, p. 208). For McFee, appreciation is 'perceptual rather than inferential' (2004, p. 213) – that is, perception of artworks does not proceed to interpretative or evaluative judgements by drawing on accepted premises or assumptions. Neither does it proceed through decoding a system of signs, as does language, say, but perception of artworks is a human capacity that is bound up in the quality of your ability *to see, to perceive, to know what to notice*. So, understanding choreographic style is subject to conventions; that is, it is bounded by rules, but they are not the same sorts of rules as those that govern language (where, for example, concept *cat* is inferred from the signifier 'cat'). Instead, understanding artworks is subject to our fitness for perception. The next step is to note that each dance discloses its own unique set of 'rules' for perception, its own mode of understanding[7]. I will now briefly tease out these ideas by returning to my previous dance example and discussing how it relates to a wider consideration of choreographic style.

Getting inside Mark Morris's *Songs that tell a story* (1982)

Analysing choreographic style, then, involves knowing what to notice in dance works, and this capacity draws on a vast array of experience: of the choreographer's other works; of her/his choreographic processes and conceptual framework; of other dance works; and of art in general (McFee 2004, p. 213). 'Robe of White' provides an interesting example of some of the problems that are typically encountered in analysing postmodern dances. To begin with, it operates, as

[7] To flesh this idea out: Crowther argues that artworks, irrespective of whether they are figurative or abstract, are primarily about the activity of perception but disclose that activity to us in a more immediate and vivid way than is normally the case. But it is in their form that artworks also disclose their own 'visual language': the unique way in which they communicate to the viewer. 'What a painting makes visible first and foremost are the conditions of its own visibility' (Crowther 1993, p. 111). That is to say, representation of the real world is subordinate to the painting's 'self-disclosure' – showing us what it is to see.

we have seen, on more than one level; but it is easy, as with other works of Mark Morris, to accept a superficial reading alone and to leave it at that. It provides an example of what Joan Acocella refers to as Morris's 'irony and sincerity' (1993, p. 183). Key to understanding Morris's work is the interplay between surface and depth – these are also familiar concerns of postmodernism. Fredric Jameson makes a distinction between pastiche and parody, which it is appropriate to deploy here, in which parody presupposes an understanding and respect for original forms, and pastiche deals in surface features alone, without understanding and, consequently, without sympathetic humour[8]. Morris *pastiches* a number of elements, but he also displays an underlying sympathy and understanding of the styles he is sending up, hence his works conform to Jameson's explanation of *parody*.

The dance is an example of Morris's earlier, pre-classically based work, in which movement vocabulary is less technically virtuosic and is drawn primarily from gesture. On the surface, the dance appears to narrate, in movement, the lyrics of its Country and Western accompaniment in a straightforward and amusing way. But I have also suggested that the dance further discusses the nature of the musical genre, or, on an even broader level, that the dance is saying something about the role of popular or folk culture in our lives. This is to claim, too, that these elements may be experienced in other of Morris's dances and that these tendencies form part of his choreographic style.

We know that Morris's dances are invariably meticulously crafted; he famously refers to himself as a 'structure queen', but dances such as the 'Waltz of the Snowflakes' from *The Hard Nut* (1991) or the opening dance of *L'Allegro, Il Penseroso ed il Moderato* (1988) display patterns of such dizzying and safety-defying complexity that this self-evaluation is amply borne out. In 'Robe of White', the organisation of the dancers in space and through time seems significant, as their changing of places on stage and their order of dancing, repetition and slight variation of gesture are features that are highlighted, alongside a play between canon and unison movement. Parallel to this apparently basic movement structure goes the interplay between emotion and mime, the development of the dance's ironic tone, and consequently the development of ideas.

In *L'Allegro* we also experience Morris's delight in musical complexity, and, more specifically to this dance, his delight in the possible relationship between words and movement. Morris finds every conceivable way of playing with words: from echoing their rhythm, to charades-style mime, to embodying the 'voice' or 'voices' of the accompaniment – for example, the '*Laudamus te*' duet in *Gloria* (1981). In *Songs* we witness many of the same features of this

[8]'Pastiche is, like parody, the imitation of a peculiar or unique style, the wearing of a stylistic mask, speech in a dead language: but it is a neutral practice of such mimicry, without parody's ulterior motive, without the satirical impulse, without laughter, without that still latent feeling that there exists something normal compared to which what is being imitated is rather comic. Pastiche is blank parody, parody that has lost its sense of humor'. Fredric Jameson (1983) 'Postmodernism and the consumer society' in Foster, H. (ed.) *Postmodern Culture*, London, Pluto, p. 114.

relationship and attitude to words. In 'Robe of White', mimetic gesture becomes more and more absurd, especially so in its relationship to the tragic tale that is unfolding in the musical accompaniment, taking on an almost surreal quality.

We know too that Morris is concerned with issues to do with humanity and the human predicament, with what one reviewer has termed the contents of 'spirituality and sexuality in equal measure', though not in a didactic way – he does not preach. In *New Love Song Waltzes* (1982), for example, Morris deals with sexual partnering in all its possible diversities, in a way that is at once tender but also finds the humour in bodily functions. Another dance that is perhaps closer in spirit to *Songs,* is *Going Away Party* (1990) choreographed to music by Bob Wills and his Texas Playboys, in which the theme of communal dancing belies an altogether darker situation, in which there is gradually disclosed an outsider at the party, who is desperate to be included. Morris created this dance during his difficult stay in Brussels.

Lastly, there is Morris's attitude to movement to take into account. He often deals with dance conventions and cultural conventions by subverting their embedded codes and undermining our assumptions about such things as the connection between movement style and gender. In *Love You Have Won* (1984), Morris places ballet alongside modern dance (and theatrical) values, thereby deconstructing the movement vocabularies but also getting us to question our preconceptions about what movement means and how it expresses what it expresses. *Songs* demonstrates a similar attitude to movement vocabulary, and Morris explores dramatic gesture, mime, pedestrian movement and modern dance, among other things, mining each for its expressive potential. But Acocella notes that 'gestures invoke not just the situations they are referring to but the whole atmosphere of the art form they are borrowed from' (1993, p. 142). The theme of the dance is clearly signalled in the title: the dance is about storytelling in dance, but as such it refers back to dance's history. So the dance in some ways may be read as being 'about' movement: its history in dance; its relation to emotion; its function within culture and society; its possibilities for expression and reference to whatever – human emotion, the human condition, archetypes and particularities. Parallel to this is its examination of the nature and function of folk culture, which in this particular instance deals with religious sentimentality. Folk is seen here as a dramatic expression of universal situations and a way of people coming to terms with grief that might otherwise devastate.

In conclusion, this essay has attempted to map a way of approaching choreographic style analysis in terms of accessing embodied ideas, without doing an injustice to the physicality – and sensuality – of the dance. It has also attempted to avoid the pitfalls inherent in many post-structuralist methodologies by suggesting boundaries to this process. Lastly, it has argued that choreographic-style analysis involves knowing what to notice, and that this process involves artistic experience and gradually acquired perceptual acuity.

First and foremost, though, it is important to remember that choreography *makes sense,* so an analysis of choreographic style has to start from an understanding of the dance: it is so much more than noting signature moves, although identifying these, of course, is also important. One way of doing this that bypasses object / subject distinctions is to employ an account of dance as embodied ideas, which then implicates dancer and viewer in the communication equation. An acknowledgement, too, that perception is dynamic, reciprocal and creative permits the concept of an active viewer, but this need not necessarily allow rampant subjectivism to come in.

Reading/Bibliography

Acocella, J. (1993) *Mark Morris*, New York, Farrar Straus Giroux.

Adshead, J., Briginshaw, V.A., Hodgens, P. and Huxley, M. (1988) *Dance Analysis: Theory and Practice,* London, Dance Books.

Adshead-Lansdale, J. (ed.) (1994) 'Dance analysis in performance', *Dance Research*, 12/2, pp. 15–20.

Adshead-Lansdale, J. (ed.) (1999) *Dancing Texts: Intertextuality in Interpretation*, London, Dance Books.

Cavell, S. (1969) 'A matter of meaning it', in *Must We Mean What We Say?*, Cambridge, Cambridge University Press, pp. 213–237.

Crowther, P. (1993) *Art and Embodiment: From Aesthetics to Self-Consciousness*, Oxford, Clarendon Press.

Crowther, P. (2003) *Philosophy After Postmodernism: Civilized Values and the Scope of Kknowledge*, London, Routledge.

Foster, S.L. (1986) *Reading Dancing: Bodies and Subjects in Contemporary American Dance*, Berkeley, Los Angeles & London, University of California Press.

Jackson, N. (1994) 'Dance analysis in the writing of Janet Adshead and Susan Foster', *Dance Research,* XII/1 Summer, pp. 3–11.

McFee, G. (1992) 'Style and technique', 'Intention and understanding', *Understanding Dance*, London, Routledge, pp. 197–213, 226–241.

McFee, G. (2004) 'Truth, dance education and the 'postmodern condition', *The Concept of Dance Education. Expanded Edition*, Eastbourne, Pageantry Press, supplementary essay 1, pp. 203–220.

Rowell, B. (2003) *An investigation into the critical analysis of postmodern dances*, unpublished PhD thesis, University of Surrey, Roehampton.

2.1.2: Issues of style in dance analysis: choreographic style or performance style?

Sarah Whatley

Analysing dances inevitably means confronting questions about dance 'style'. Whether the dance is viewed live in performance, recorded on film or notated, a close reading by the initiated observer should help to identify distinctive features, which may reveal clues about dance style. For example, consider what it is that characterises the bold physicality of William Forsythe's somewhat unconventional and convoluted choreographic style. Contrast that with what makes Rosemary Butcher's more minimalist, meditative and poetic work and then compare that with the ingredients of Lea Anderson's quirky, gestural, witty choreographic style. But is style created by the choreographer, independent of the performers and irrespective of context, or does it result from a more complex relationship between those who create the dance and the dancers' contributions and interpretations of dance material?

In this essay, consideration will be given to what is meant by dance style and what may be a subtle but important distinction between what can be regarded as 'choreographic style' and 'performance style'. On the one hand, 'performance style' may refer to different forms, types or genres of performance that can be said to share something in common (for example, ballet, tango or hip-hop) although the multiplicity of styles, and the cross-over between different styles today means that this is not straightforward. But it may also refer to the style of the performers that either individually or collectively establishes a performance style for the work in question or discrete body of works. Here again, however, the role and contribution of the dancer in the creative process varies widely between and within dance forms. Some dancers may be required to learn patterns of movement as set by the choreographer, with little opportunity for creative input during the construction stage. Alternatively, dancers may contribute much to the creation of dance material, acting more as the 'agents' of the choreographer. In this case the choreographer may well be in more of a directorial role, editing and shaping the dancers' material.

When investigating any established choreographer's body of works, the viewer will probably be drawn to those characteristics that seem to recur across works, as well as significant differences between works. Characteristics may be related to the choreographic processes and devices, which give rise to what may appear to be codes and vocabularies. The dancers then embody codes and vocabularies in particular ways, not only in each choreography but also in each and every performance. Consideration may also be given to elements outside the movement itself: to the design, to the treatment of sound or music and so on. When taken as a whole, these characteristics probably go some way towards determining a choreographic style. Of course, the viewer is inevitably drawing from personal experience and taste to make judgements, so it is important to acknowledge that the viewer also has a role in determining style. In that sense, judgments can never be truly objective, although different viewers, writers and critics may reach some agreement. The choreographer may well also have opinions about his or her own style, which will probably influence judgements. But any investigation of a particular choreographer's dance style will benefit from exploring the idea of 'style' itself.

What is dance style?

Many dance writers have contemplated the complexities of style in relation to dance. Susan Leigh Foster proposes that 'style results from three related sets of choreographic conventions: the quality with which the movement is performed, the characteristic use of parts of the body, and the dancer's orientation in the performance space' (1986, p. 77). She later proposes that style 'washes over the entire vocabulary of a dance, giving it a cultural and individual identity' (1986, p. 91). Adina Armelagos and Mary Sirridge, on the other hand, claim that 'style is the most important concept we can use to understand dance' (1984, p. 86), suggesting that style is a twofold concept (1984, p. 86). Armelagos and Sirridge make an important distinction between general style, which they describe as produced by a spatial vocabulary – an inventory of allowable positions and movement sequences held together by a system of kinesthetic motivation – and personal style, described as the dancer's particular contribution within general style (1978, p. 131). But they suggest it is only through understanding general style that a dancer develops a personal style (1984, p. 90). In their view, personal style is therefore both an articulation and a further development of general style (1978, p. 131). Personal style, in this context, could be seen to be analogous to performance style, and general style analogous to choreographic style, and the dancer is regarded as having an active role in contributing to style.

Attending to the dancers' contribution to each and any version of a dance can, however, be viewed as problematic. For example, Janet Adshead-Lansdale (1999), in consideration of how dances can be interpreted, draws attention to the problem of attempting to distinguish not only the choreographer but also the performer and reader from the dance. She proposes that one way of dealing with the problem is to deny the existence of the performer, dissolving the performer into the dance, seeing it all as text, suggesting that distinctions between creator, performer and reader can be regarded as either redundant or suspiciously positivistic (1999, p. 4). This tension or what Sheets-Johnstone and Richardson describe as the 'process/product dichotomy' (1984, pp. 63) between the dance 'text' as object and the role of the dancers is why it is always difficult to judge the extent to which the dancers themselves influence or create performance style. It may be the case that the relationship put forward by Armelagos and Sirridge is not so straightforward, and the dancer's personal style develops alongside but in sympathy with the choreographer's general style. Furthermore, what is known about particular dancers and their role in the construction of the dance may well provide a useful insight into style, and performance style in particular. Indeed, as Armelagos and Sirridge point out themselves, choreographers will frequently draw on the dancers' natural proclivities and abilities to shape their work (1978, p. 133). Of course, when the choreographer and dancer are one and the same (described by Armelagos and Sirridge as the 'autonomous choreographer' [1984, pp. 91–92]) then differentiating between choreographic style and personal style becomes problematic, as each originates and develops simultaneously. These varying perspectives offer different routes into contemplating dance style, and one choreographer whose choreographic output provides a useful model to explore some of the issues raised here is Siobhan Davies.

Siobhan Davies

Siobhan Davies (1950–), widely recognised as one of Britain's most important choreographers, has created over 50 works for Britain's major dance companies. Although she has been influenced by the work of other choreographers, as well as by new directions and trends in British and American dance in a more general sense, her work has assumed its own very particular stylistic identity.

Since 1988, Davies's choreographic style has embodied a number of recurring values. These include a multidirectional, sequential, segmented use of body parts; a sensing of the internal space of the body; an easy musculature and weighted quality; and an easy passage of movement into and away from the floor. Thus Davies's style emerges through her own particular approach to working with time and space. But key to Davies's working method is the freedom she gives each dancer in her company to colour the movement differently, particular to the dancer's own bodily structure. Furthermore, she invites her dancers to bring their personal qualities to the dance, to encourage each individual to find convincing, 'real' movement that they own, rather than having movement imposed upon them. She has views about how each of her dancers contributes different qualities, 'problems', and a different history to the dance[9]. Therefore, and in common with a number of other contemporary choreographers, Davies seems to want her dancers to take authorship of their roles within her dances, regarding their own interpretation as important. Davies's choreographic method seems to support Ann Cooper Albright's claim that dance performances are 'extreme examples of a fluidity of authorship' (1997, p. 186). But according to Graham McFee, a dance cannot be confronted in any way other than in an 'interpreted' form, so the performer's interpretation does not really constitute a level of interpretation at all (1992, p. 124). McFee's view may challenge the point made by Albright, but returns to Adshead-Lansdale's point about the need to dissolve the performers into the dance and see all as one text.

Davies's working process appears to diminish any distinction between the choreography and the dancers, as separate from or as interpreters of the choreography. To this extent, perhaps her dances should not be confronted as an 'interpreted' form. But knowing the different ways in which individual dancers do contribute to the dance inevitably informs any views about the way in which Davies's choreographic style has developed. A brief examination of one of Davies's most popular works, *Winnsboro Cotton Mill Blues* (1992), illustrates well how not only choreographic style but performance style emerges from and influences the analytic process.

[9] Any views or comments attributed to Davies in this essay are drawn from conversations and interviews with her over the period 1989–2000.

Winnsboro Cotton Mill Blues

The concept for *Winnsboro Cotton Mill Blues* developed from piano music composed by the American composer Fredric Rzewski (1979), from which the title of the dance is taken[10]. A working environment, and particularly that of the southern states of America, is established in the nexus of movement, sound and design. Davies makes reference to factory work in the gestural movement for the hands and also in floor patterns created by dancers moving predominantly in straight lines (across the stage or on the diagonal) and occasionally in circles, like wheels. What is of particular interest in the context of this essay is that *Winnsboro Cotton Mill Blues* was first choreographed for Rambert Dance Company in 1992 and reworked for her own company, Siobhan Davies Dance Company, in 1998. Discussion will thus consider the extent to which each version contributes to an understanding of Davies's style.

Whilst the analysis here focuses principally on the dance itself, it also takes into account three interrelated sub-strands of enquiry. These are Davies's changing choreographic method between the first and later version, her developing approach to the moving body and also Davies's relationship to her dancers and the different ways in which they are able to contribute to the choreography. Each sub-strand can provide a different entry point to the dance, and taken together provide a richer analysis as well as tools for comparing this dance with other dances by Davies. By looking in detail at how the movement changes from one version to the next, and by acknowledging the different perspectives that are brought to bear on the analysis, style may be embodied differently in each version; but taken together, there is something unmistakeably 'Davies' in this choreography[11].

Davies's original choreography for *Winnsboro Cotton Mill Blues* developed out of choreographic tasks that she set, which grew partly out of her interest in imagining what workers in mills may be thinking whilst working, and partly out of the movement of the machines[12]. The resultant movement was therefore generated largely by the dancers themselves. In reworking, Davies deliberately took the dancers through the same choreographic process as she used in the 'original'[13], meaning that, although much of the dance structure remained unchanged in the revival, much of the dancers' movement is different. This is because each group of dancers relied on what was more familiar to them in terms of dance vocabulary and choreographic experience.

[10] *Winnsboro Cotton Mill Blues* is Rzewski's name for the fourth and last of his solo piano pieces entitled *North American Ballads*.

[11] No notated score of the dance is available; but if it were, it would allow the reader to detect the extent to which style is encoded in the notation, and would also allow for more comparisons to be made between the different versions of the dance.

[12] Pre-performance talk, The Swan Theatre, High Wycombe, May 6 1998.

[13] Inverted commas are used here to indicate that although the reference is to the first production of this choreography, the notion of an 'original' version is more complicated, because it could suggest that this version has more validity or authority than any other version.

When it was first performed, *Winnsboro Cotton Mill Blues* was viewed by many as more extrovert and energetic than Davies's work for her own company at this time, maybe because the original dancers, used to performing in large-scale theatres, gave an outwardly focused performance. In contrast to Davies's own company, the Rambert dancers' technical training at that time included (in addition to Richard Alston's contemporary technique) classical ballet technique, emphasising verticality and the sense of 'arrival'. The dancers inevitably brought this body-knowledge to their dancing (see diagram 1).

Since 1988, Davies's reluctance to choreograph 'steps'[14] in favour of exploring a movement vocabulary that emphasises motion and the flow of movement is manifested differently in the two versions of the dance. The Rambert Dance Company dancers make clearer the distinction between walking, running, gesturing and, in particular, the more elevated, danced 'steps'. The dancers invest more 'attack' and presentation in these steps, appearing confident with material more familiar to them. Davies comments on this, believing that her aim of making the piece relevant for the dancers in her own company was partly realised in her decision to remove what she described as the 'repertory steps'[15]. According to Davies, these repertory steps and other movement ideas became incorporated into the original choreography through a lack of rehearsal time. For example, in the revival turning is always the result of another part of the body motivating movement. Turns become connecting movement, skimming the floor, whereas in the 'original', turns are danced more upright, more vertically, emphasising the upward motion in the torso, drawing attention to the turn as an isolated movement.

In both versions, the dancers hold their own limbs and body parts of other dancers, suggesting the need for human contact. In the 'original', the holding of limbs appears more functional. In the revival, more trust and comfort is implied. The dancers are more practised in sharing weight, so the quality of touch appears different. Davies's dancers respond to gravity with weighty swings and a flow of movement throughout the whole body, producing the effect that they use their weight differently from the original dancers. It also points to Davies's growing interest at that time in how movement in one part of the body influences movement in another.

The choreography includes more falls onto the floor than leaps and jumps away from the floor, but elevation in the 'original' is made more aerial. The dancers extend their legs high into space to travel upwards and along the floor, with stretched feet. The dancers' focus is into the line of direction, and energy in the whole body is directed into moving the body forwards. The dynamic shape of the movement is plainer, gathering inwards before exploding outwards. Davies's own dancers occupy space differently. Although they cover the stage space with energy

[14] In this context, the notion of 'steps' refers to those units of movement that are separable, repeatable, and identifiable as actions that have spatial and rhythmic form (Preston-Dunlop 1998, p. 95). This notion is often associated with 'codified' steps, those which 'belong' to existing dance vocabularies.

[15] 'Repertory steps' in this context are understood to mean those 'steps' that can be identified and named, which frequently recur across different works by different choreographers, and are often practised regularly in class, thereby becoming a potential resource for choreography.

similar to that of the original dancers, vertical space is neutralised. With few 'repertory steps', which specifically, by their definition, take the dancer into the air, or onto the floor, the dynamic range in the revival is less extreme. Yet, on the other hand, the increased bodily articulation of the dancers draws out more rhythmic interest and the perception of increased complexity and attention to smaller, detailed movement.

Diagram 1: *Winnsboro Cotton Mill Blues* (1992): different dancers and the impact on Davies' choreographic style.

1992 version (Rambert Dance Company)	**1998 version (Siobhan Davies Dance Company)**
More 'attack', outward projection and focus	Softer gaze
Incorporation of 'repertory' steps	Fluid connections, removing 'repertory steps'; emphasis on passage of movement
Isolated, separated turns within dance phrases	Turns as connecting or transitional movement within dance phrases
Functional touch	Different quality of touch; trust, comfort, warmth
Less fluid use of weight	More weighty swings/flow/giving in to gravity
More aerial elevation, more 'upward' energy, plainer	Vertical space neutralised in moving into and away from the floor
Few 'body designs' but emphasis on spatial patterning in space and in the body	Increased bodily articulation, giving more rhythmic interest/complexity and emphasis on dynamic structures or properties

The changes evident in the revival may result from Davies having a clearer notion of what her original intention was. But working with dancers who were more experienced in working collaboratively with her, who were more familiar with her aesthetic vision and were confident with imprinting their own personality on the work, must also have a bearing on the changes. Consequently, even those aspects of the choreography that are the 'same' in both versions demonstrate how the different dancers in each version affect the movement vocabulary, that either results from or gives rise to a different performance style. Developments and changes perceived in the later version thus result partly from the dancers' own interpretation or re-interpretation of the original choreography, and partly from their contribution to the creation of new choreography. In broad terms, the 'original' emphasises spatial patterning, the revival emphasises dynamic and rhythmic characteristics. Hence the performance style of the dancers in her own company means that the revival is more recognisably Davies's post-1988 choreographic style.

Links to other dances in Davies's repertoire provide further clues to what constitutes Davies's style. The reference to America in the thematic content and music recurs several times after 1988 and the urban, industrial theme is returned to in *Eighty Eight* (1998), which was toured alongside the revised *Winnsboro Cotton Mill Blues*. The work gestures for the hands link to gestures in many other choreographies[16], making clear how Davies regards the hands and arms as the most expressive part of the body for the dancer (cited in Thrift 1996, p. 10). Partnering work is characterised by the dancers in her own company working with a responsive body, informed by a perception of touch, weight and momentum, indicating a collective activity. Several choreographic devices also recur and the clear spatial patterns and formations characterise many of her works. A particular recurring choreographic device is the 'unclimactic' ending. Davies frequently draws a dance to a close with the dancers still moving as the lights darken or the music ends, communicating the idea of the human body in continual motion. This device also invites the viewer to anticipate or imagine what may follow, connecting one dance to the next. Another linking characteristic is the shift to working from the principle of releasing muscular tension, to finding ways of allowing greater articulation in the body, producing a softer, more rounded effect.

It can thus be seen that the treatment of the constituent features of the dance (action, space, dynamics, relationships, thematic ideas, music, design and so on) and how these features combine to formulate recurring themes and devices (for example, the unclimactic ending) establish some stylistic traits that connect this choreography to Davies's entire body of work. But the extent to which the properties that are the dance exist beyond the dancer, and the extent to which an individual dancer's history not only determines his or her own personal performance style but colours a choreographer's choreographic style is what is of interest. The dance, as a text, is the primary object for discussion, but the changing role and responsibilities of the dancers are arguably an important contributing factor to style.

Davies is the first to acknowledge the contribution of her dancers to her choreography.

[16] *Signature* (1990), *Different Trains* (1990), *Make-Make* (1992), *The Art of Touch* (1995), *A Stranger's Taste* (1999) and *Plants and Ghosts* (2002) are all examples. A more detailed examination of the use of gesture in Davies's choreography is provided in Whatley (2002).

Some of her dancers have worked with her for many years, having a significant influence on the way her work has developed, and have even become synonymous with Davies's choreography. Gill Clarke, for example, has retained a close working relationship with Davies since 1988. Davies describes Clarke as exhibiting a profound sense of 'through knowledge' in her entire body, with all parts of the body employed in any one movement. The partnership has been extraordinarily productive and Clarke has created many roles. But Davies's method ensures that the dancer dancing at that particular time at once owns a role, however apparently closely related to a previous version or performance of that role. As such, a 'role' is therefore a fluid concept in Davies's choreography and respects the particularity of each dancer's bodily conformation. Once again it appears that Davies's choreography is indivisible from those who perform it.

Comparing one dancer's performance with another in Davies's choreography is likely to bring few rewards, whereas a comparison of the overall effect created by a different quality of movement as executed by all the dancers collectively, as discussed in relation to *Winnsboro Cotton Mill Blues,* can lead to different interpretations of the dance and conclusions about choreographic style. However, Gill Clarke does have particular movement qualities, which can be identified in different dances. These qualities 'help shape the dancer's own performance persona – a theatrical version of the dancer's personality' (Foster 1986, p. 77). To this extent, Clarke's personal style can have an important influence, helping to establish the identity of the dance. But there are other examples where this infusion of personal style can seem to detract from the choreographer's style. To take one example, Rudolph Nureyev's performance in Martha Graham's choreography raised a number of questions, not only about the 'balletisation' of the choreography of one of the great 'moderns' but also about the impact Nureyev's distinctive performance style had on Graham's well-established style. It appeared that Nureyev's personal style dominated, leading to what could be described as a 'stylistically deviant' (Armelagos and Sirridge 1978, p. 134) performance of Graham's choreography.

Not only the dancing but the dancing body itself has influence on choreographic style. A reading of Balanchine's choreography, or indeed Cunningham's, may be very different if the body of the dancers is different. A sense of uniformity in body type contributes to the identification of the style in both these choreographers' work. By contrast, in the case of Mark Morris, it is the diversity of body type that gives rise to the style characteristics of Morris's choreography. The emergence of choreographers and dancers who develop their own style through a preparedness to disrupt dance conventions and ideas of conformity and attend to a 'flexibility of movement identities' (Albright 2001, p. 65) ensures that searching for style characteristics is not a straightforward endeavour. So, is the task to identify stylistic traits in one work that seem to colour other work by the same choreographer? Or is it to look for broader style characteristics that identify the work as belonging to a broader genre, trend or milieu? Is it to look for elements in the dance that seem to signal change or deviation from a previous stylistic form? And what is it that determines the concordance or change? Where does the responsibility for style lie: in the dancer, the choreographer, the audience, the critic?

In simple but perplexing terms: do the dancers embody style or is style embodied in the dancers? These and other questions will inevitably give rise to many varied views and opinions, which ensures that the debate, like dance itself, is a live and changing one, contingent on those who create, perform and view the dance.

The relationship between performance style and choreographic style may well be fluid and particular to different dances and different choreographers or genres. And any distinction between these concepts of style, however subtle, can be both illuminated and confused by a functioning dialogic relationship between the choreographed and the performed. But one way of looking at the relationship is to regard 'choreographic style' as that which can be said to be established by and pertaining to one choreographer, as evident in a body of works by the choreographer and embodied by different dancers, and probably spanning across time. Links can, however, be usefully made between the choreographic style of different choreographers. Although not entirely independent of choreographic style, performance style can refer to an identifiable style of presentation, created by an individual performer or collectively by the performers in one work or a body of work. This interconnectedness emerges as a matrix, a kind of 'style fabric' in which choreographer, dancer, tradition and convention are woven together to construct something particular and essential that has colour, texture and longevity. It follows therefore that the extent to which dance style, in all its many manifestations, can be observed, documented and worked into or reconstructed from notation is one of the many challenges of the analytic process.

Reading/Bibliography

Adshead-Lansdale, J. (ed.) (1999) *Dancing Texts: Intertextuality in Interpretation*, London, Dance Books.

Albright, A.C. (1997) 'Auto-body stories: Blondell Cummings and autobiography in dance', in J. Desmond (ed.) *Meaning in Motion: New Cultural Studies of Dance*, Durham (North Carolina) and London, Duke University Press.

Albright, A.C. (2001) 'Strategic abilities: Negotiating the disabled body in dance', in A. Dils & A.C. Albright (eds) *Moving History/Dancing Cultures: A Dance History Reader*, Durham (North Carolina), Wesleyan University Press.

Armelagos, A. & Sirridge, M. (1978) 'The identity crisis in dance', *Journal of Aesthetics and Arts Criticism*, 37/1 Winter, pp. 129–141.

Armelagos, A. & Sirridge, M. (1984) 'Personal style and performance prerogatives' in M. Sheets-Johnstone (ed.) *Illuminating Dance: Philosophical Explorations,* London, Associated University Press.

Foster, S.L. (1986) *Reading Dancing: Bodies and Subjects in Contemporary American Dance*, California, University of California Press.

McFee, G. (1992) *Understanding Dance*, London, Routledge.

Preston-Dunlop, V. (1998) *Looking at Dances: a Choreological Perspective on Choreography*, Ightham, Verve Publishing.

Sheets-Johnstone, M. & Richardson, D. (1984) 'Dance, Whitehead, and Faustian II themes' in M. Sheets-Johnstone (ed.) *Illuminating Dance: Philosophical Explorations*, London, Associated University Press.

Thrift, J. (ed.) (1996) *Siobhan Davies in Residence Seminar Programme*, London, Roehampton Institute.

Whatley, S. (2002) *Beneath the Surface: the Movement Vocabulary in Siobhan Davies' Choreography since 1988*, unpublished PhD thesis, University of Surrey, Roehampton.

Acknowledgements

I should like to thank Jane Pritchard, Archivist for Rambert Dance Company, for providing access to the video recording of the Rambert Dance Company production of *Winnsboro Cotton Mill Blues*; and Siobhan Davies for her generosity in allowing me to see much of this choreography in rehearsal and for discussing her work with me.

2.1.3: Dancing off the page? Notation and its challenges

Rachel Duerden

Twenty years ago, a US university teacher, Judy van Zile, wrote:

> Many people complain that movement notation is complicated and too cumbersome to take time to learn. I have continually argued that it is no more complicated than the movement it documents, and that the teaching of dance notation is also the teaching of skill in visual perception. We now wait to teach notation until our dancers are fairly advanced in their movement training. They are no longer interested in analyzing, recording, or reading in notation a basic triplet when they are spending their time mastering the performance intricacies of a spiral fall or a complex adagio sequence. But the notation of the basic triplet is simple – perhaps even simpler than the movement itself when it is first taught to beginning-level students. And if the student possessed the theoretical understanding and visual acuity that go hand in hand with learning notation, the fall or adagio might be easier to master. (van Zile 1985–6, p. 45)

This problem is a familiar one to many dance teachers who use, or want to use, notation; today we might speak in terms of wanting to encourage in students an 'embodied understanding', meaning the bodily intelligence that a dancer learns to develop and that a knowledge of the conceptual frameworks of notation can facilitate. Some of my own best and most vivid memories of being an undergraduate are of working with a score and gradually, very gradually, beginning to understand what the choreographer was 'getting at', by learning how to embody that choreography myself. That is the key issue: developing a bodily intelligence and an embodied understanding, skills that dancers – more than any other professionals, perhaps – have the potential to achieve. Studying a score does focus the attention on the detail as well as the larger picture: detail that is frequently lost or misinterpreted in watching video or film, for example, but that can hold the key to full embodied understanding as the dancer works at achieving the subtleties as well as the overall shape and 'flow'.

The underlying focus of this book is the relationship between score and dance in its many manifestations, and a number of important philosophical issues are implicit in the various discussions and approaches that have been introduced. I should like now to consider some of these in a little more detail, and with reference to writers and theorists as well as practitioners, whose thinking and practice have contributed to the debate as a whole and serve to throw further light on the issues themselves.

The notated dance score shares important similarities with a music score or a play-text – offering a sense of the author's intentions but requiring reconstruction and interpretation. Both these terms – 'reconstruction' and 'interpretation' – are rather loaded, philosophically speaking, but my point here is that dance, music and theatre all become manifest as artworks through performance. The importance of the score or text is understood in relation to drama and music, but sometimes seems to be regarded with suspicion in dance, as if notating a dance inevitably restricts its dynamic existence and pins it down to a single interpretation (although in fact the danger of this is much greater if film or video is the only documentary medium). So in the course of this investigation of the relationship between score and dance, I should like also to consider some possible reasons for the problems that people sometimes see in that relationship – to look at some of the perceived difficulties with dance notation, and to offer some different perspectives.

The main areas of debate in this context are documentation and authenticity, history, reconstruction and revival, and understanding dance both intellectually and physically (or embodied knowledge). The last of those is, of course, the major concern of this book, but the others are equally important in the wider debate about dance notation and its relationship to choreography.

Documentation and authenticity (1)

One of the most contentious issues in this debate concerns the capacity of any notation system to capture, adequately and faithfully, the intentions of the creator: to represent the 'authentic' work. In this context, it is helpful to consider other performing arts whose continuing existence requires documentation or notation of some kind.

Music

If we first make comparison with music: music scores are recognised to be very much sketches of the musical intention, ranging from graphic scores with instructions to the performer (like stage directions) to the conventional orchestral score that includes pitches, rhythms, orchestration, phrasing, dynamic and speed. The relationship between the dot on the page and the sound produced is very flimsy in some respects, but this does not seem to present a problem to musicians – perhaps because the composer is (unlike the choreographer) also the notator and the score is in fact 'the result of the creative process' (Youngerman 1984, p. 102)[17]. However, even the composer needs the performer to bring the music to the audience. Judy van Zile quotes Igor Stravinsky:

> It is taken for granted that I place before the performer written music wherein the composer's will is explicit and easily discernible from a correctly established text. But no matter how scrupulously a piece of music may be notated, no matter how carefully it may be insured against every possible ambiguity through indications of *tempo*, shading, phrasing, accentuation, and so on, it always contains hidden elements that defy definition because verbal dialectic is powerless to define musical dialectic in its totality. The realization of these elements is thus a matter of experience and intuition, in a word, of the talent of the person who is called upon to present the music. (Stravinsky 1959, in van Zile 1985–6, p. 45)

[17] 'How can I know what I think till I see what I write?' (attributed to E.M. Forster, in Webb, E. [1987] 'English as aesthetic initiative', in P. Abbs [ed.], *Living Powers: The Arts in Education,* Lewes, The Falmer Press, pp. 69–97). The dance equivalent of 'writing' is more likely to be the *creation* of movement material in the studio than the *notating* of that material, but the relationship between the creative idea and its tangible realisation similarly involves experiment, testing, critical analysis and conceptualisation.

Stravinsky here is clearly acknowledging the central importance of the performer, whose 'experience and intuition' inform the performance itself: another way of defining embodied knowledge, perhaps. It is interesting to note, however, that some composers have, in more recent years, developed comprehensively detailed notations and graphic scores, instructing the player when to breathe, how to stand, how to hold the instrument and so on, and challenging the capacity for 'dots on the page' to represent the subtleties of soundscape they wish to capture and convey. This could appear to be an attempt to overcome even that level of interpretation that Stravinsky saw as inevitable, but perhaps it is more to the point that a notation system must be capable of adaptation and development in response to the needs of the creative artist.

Allographical versus autographical

The disputed role of notation in the documentation of dance raises questions about the status of dance as either an 'allographic' or an 'autographic' art form. The story of twentieth-century modern dance includes many examples of practitioners such as Martha Graham whose performances of their own work became apparently inseparable from those works, so far did the creator/performers imprint their own personality and interpretation upon the work. This appears to lead to a position where the choreography is seen as 'autographic', rather than 'allographic'; in other words, only the choreographer's 'version' or performance is the true work, and every other interpretation is a pale imitation. But most people, I suspect, are more likely to accept that dance is allographic rather than autographic, and thus shares more with music and other performing arts than with, for example, visual art. 'In the [autographic arts]… there can only be one original (even a brilliant forgery of *The Mona Lisa* is just that: a forgery). But for the allographic arts like music (and presumably, dance) no single performance (not even the first performance) can ever be definitive' (Copeland 1994, p. 19). It is this last comment in parentheses that is likely to provoke debate, especially in those cases where either the choreographer or a 'special' dancer or muse becomes very closely identified with the work.

In recent times, choreographers have frequently made work for specific dancers and very much with those dancers' personalities and performance qualities in mind, as Sarah Whatley discusses in her essay. It may be argued that the dance, in its first incarnation, is forever lost once the original dancers no longer perform it. This is, on certain significant levels, true, of course; dance does not enjoy a persistent identity in the way that a painting does. But that first incarnation can *never* be recreated, and this applies equally to every dance performance. Graham McFee (1992) argues, like Copeland, that even the first performance of a choreography is not the definitive dance, but only the first of – potentially – many 'versions' of it. As a performing art, however, dance has the potential for a dynamic existence: ever changing, but capable of living through those changes. New performers can re-invigorate the work and bring new insights to it, as has frequently been demonstrated, especially in theatre and in music.

Returning to the comparison with music notation: Labanotation is, arguably, far more detailed than musical notation, giving instructions about *how* to perform as well as *what* to perform at every level. This can be seen as a problem, especially in relation to the issue of 'definitive' performances on the one hand and new 'interpretations' on the other. Notation can be seen as being *too* detailed and prescriptive and thus not allowing for individual interpretation. Paradoxically, while it can thus be seen as over-detailed, at the same time it may be criticised for failing to capture a key aspect: the human 'nuances' that are so impossible to define and yet seen as somehow 'essential' to the work. These are precisely those apparently indefinable qualities that are embodied by the dancer who is identified so closely with the work.

But we have seen (in Part 1, in 'Reading and reconstruction' and 'Analysing choreographic style') that the notator is already interpreting the choreographer's intentions through the choices made about how to record the movement (perhaps this perceived problem would be resolved when the choreographer and the notator are one and the same), and is therefore taking account of much more than just 'mechanical' movements. Decisions need to be made about *how* a movement is achieved, not simply what it looks like. Rudolf von Laban himself explained the underlying principle of Labanotation by drawing attention to the difference between the outer image and the inner workings of a wheel: 'The representation of a wheel by a circle gives its outer form as it is seen from the outside, so to speak. The representation of the wheel by the spokes shows us the inner tension forces which keep the wheel spokes apart. The wheel is seen from within here.' (Laban in Youngerman 1984, p. 114)

Theatre

Another form of capturing a performance art on paper is, of course, the play-text and, as in music, it is likely that the creator and the notator/writer are one and the same person. Anyone who can read has instant access to hundreds of plays. However, play-texts have for generations been seen as *starting points* for directors to build their own newly created work from – it is expected and even required that each new director will approach the work anew and consider interpretative options. There is a similar relationship between the text and the performance of a theatre piece to the relationship between the dance score and performance of a choreography, and the traditions of each performance art share the convention of the passing-on of ideas from one generation to the next. As theatre director Richard Schechner says: 'Theatre has both an oral and a written tradition ... Each 'doing' of a play is an interpretation, a recasting of the written tradition in the ongoing terms of the oral tradition ... Because theatre is 'done', productions which radically interpret a text are not only plausible but inevitable.' (In van Zile 1985–6, p. 43)

Despite the imaginative efforts of a number of dance practitioners (see Ann Hutchinson), for most of Western theatre dance's history the major means of preserving dances has been the equivalent of the oral tradition in theatre: that is, passing knowledge on to the next generation through teaching and demonstration. Perhaps because of the absence of a score that could be referred to as in some sense definitive, the dance tradition has also, on many occasions, allowed for much more than just slight variations among productions, with choreographers re-writing major sections or even almost the entire work, and re-framing the work in terms of setting, period and so on.[18].

Idealist or materialist?

We come thus to another focus of debate in the arts: with each new performance, how much is it permissible to change? What are the 'constants' that *must* be kept the same? In music, one might argue, the notes are the constant (or the 'constituent' rather than the 'contingent', to borrow from Goodman). But in dance, if we consider, for example, two versions of *Swan Lake*, can we say that the 'steps' are the constant feature? Referring to Jack Anderson's theory, Roger Copeland writes '[t]he idealist believes that the essence of the work resides in a concept or intention ... The materialist by contrast believes that the steps themselves are sacrosanct, but that anything (and everything) else can be changed' (Copeland 1994, p. 19). Both of these positions beg further questions: for example, if we looked at Martha Graham's solo *Lamentation* from the materialist view, would that then mean that we could dispense with the costume that stretches with the dancer, creating shapes and tensions that are, arguably, inseparable from the choreography? If we take the idealist model, on the other hand, how can we know what counts as 'the concept or intention' behind the work? Sarah Rubidge (1995) offers, as illustration of this latter issue, the famous virtuoso Black Swan solo in *Swan Lake* with the 32 *fouetté* turns. Now that this is something achievable by many dancers, rather than a dazzling technical feat attainable only by a few, then it does seem plausible to suggest that an alternative virtuoso step, reflecting the technical standards of the day and creating an equally dazzling image of the character, could be appropriate to substitute for something that is now standard. But where do we draw the line? And without access to a documentation of the 'original', how can we begin to judge whether or not, or to what extent, we are remaining true to the original intention?

These are indeed knotty problems, but they bring us back to the role of the reconstructor, whose responsibility extends beyond a straightforward competence in reading notation. The term 'reconstructor' is itself somewhat problematic, since it seems to imply a kind of assembling of separate parts, like a jigsaw or a child's model plane kit, which in turns seems to rule out any particularly creative involvement or decision-making. But of course that is not the case for the dance reconstructor, who must be both rigorous in reading the score, and informed, imaginative and intuitive when engaging with the materials, in order to mount something that is recognisably a dance, rather than an exercise in score-reading. The reconstructor needs to have a sense of the history of the work, in fact.

[18] It is interesting to consider the amount of freedom that is allowed in working with music scores and play-texts, and the extent to which the fact that dance deals with the human body in motion – not, primarily, either with spoken words or with instruments – is a significant factor in this debate.

History, reconstruction and revival

As mentioned above, choreographers generally work with real human bodies in the space when they choreograph, and thus with those real dancers' idiosyncrasies and personalities, embedding these things in the work itself, as do choreographer/dancers such as Martha Graham, as we have seen (see also Sarah Whatley's essay above). It is sometimes suggested that these aspects are too elusive for score-writing, and too important to be left to chance. But there is, arguably, something in choreography that goes beyond what *that* particular body is doing in the space; another human body may 'embody' the choreography equally well and, arguably, by doing so, throw new light on it. Muriel Topaz, notator and reconstructor, certainly believed this: 'If the choreographic art exists, then it must do so as more than a vehicle for the performer, no matter how virtuosic, stylistically pure or finely honed ... And, if it exists ... it must survive changing tastes, changing technical training and changes in the eye of the beholder' (in Copeland 1994, p. 19). Not only must it survive changes in taste and so on – it must, above all, *survive*, pure and simple.

'We need to ask what price young choreographers pay when (unlike aspiring painters or composers) they have little or no opportunity to study and absorb past masterworks in a systematic way' (Copeland 1994, p. 18). Although there is no substitute for seeing the work itself in performance, this is not sufficient to allow for systematic study. Copeland also points out that, even should the argument be put forward that a film or video could record a choreographer's intention more faithfully, this would never be acceptable in another discipline as the sole means of preserving the work for future performers and audiences. 'What actor in his right mind would want to "learn" the role of Stanley Kowalski solely by watching Marlon Brando in the film version of *Streetcar named Desire*? Can we even imagine a pianist who would learn Chopin's *Twelve Etudes* solely by listening to a recording of Artur Rubinstein performing them?' (Copeland 1994, p. 19)

The challenge, then, is to negotiate the tensions between what we believe to be the most important features of the work – perhaps an underlying concept or intention (the ideas they embody) – and to ensure their continued existence, and what we believe to be important in performance, namely fresh, insightful interpretations that ensure that the work 'lives' as more than a historical oddity.

Authenticity and the living work

Authenticity is a word that crops up in many different contexts, and frequently in the performing arts. An 'authentic music' performance will probably be played on 'period' instruments – earlier versions of the familiar orchestral instruments of today, giving different sounds and resonances. An 'authentic' performance of a Shakespeare play might require a theatrical setting close to that of the Globe Theatre, and without the modern accoutrements of lighting and other theatrical effects. There is a delicate path to be trodden here, however. The importance of contextual understanding and sensitivity can scarcely be overstated, but at the same time it is crucial that the critical eye is not dimmed; in other words, the work must be seen as a living work, rather than a museum piece, for example.[19] It may be that underlying some of the resistance to dance notation is an anxiety about this very issue, and a concern that the score may become more important than the 'living' danced work.

Sometimes an objection is raised about notated scores because many choreographers like to return to earlier works and re-work them. But this is surely no problem – composers and playwrights and novelists do the same. Having recorded a work in notation once does not preclude the possibility of returning to it and revising it. In fact it *facilitates* that, because it is not necessary to rely on memory in order to consider what one did before.

It can be most interesting to see different versions of the same work, to chart its development and change, and to glean new insights as a result. Excellent and very illuminating examples of this can be seen in Stephanie Jordan's video (2002). Here we can see not only different performances of the same work, showing how styles change over time, but also how choreographers and composers can sometimes choose to go back to earlier works and revise them. Both Balanchine and Stravinsky, in their respective fields of dance and music, frequently returned to earlier works to revise, modify and edit them. This can offer wonderful insights into the creative process and the development of an artistic voice, as well as insights into the historical trajectory.

Documentation and authenticity (2)

A fairly common misconception is the notion that notation can only record mechanical actions (forward low, side middle etc.). This probably reflects the illiteracy of the dance community more than anything else, and the fact that many dance people have had some experience of notation but not got much further than a very elementary level! (Hence this workbook, of course.)[20]

Student dancers beginning to learn notation frequently start with basic movements of walking in different directions and at different levels (but only three of each), and then moving

[19] Richard Taruskin, musicologist, argues the importance of a music performance working *as music* for today's audience, and he warns against blinding ourselves to that in the search for historical 'authenticity': 'The establishment of a work as authentic can take the place of authentic critical judgement of it' (Taruskin 1995, p. 69). The danger, as he sees it, is that deciding exactly what the author intended becomes more important than realising a living performance of a work – one that speaks to us now, today, in the way that art does. Although the situation is very different in dance, in that we have very few scores to pore over and establish the authenticity of at all, the point about the living work is well made, and applicable across the arts.

[20] I suspect that the occasional prejudice against notation is more to do with the facts that a) most dancers are notation-illiterate, and therefore understandably suspicious and possibly defensive; b) notated scores are so few, comparatively speaking, that they are seen as anomalous – unusual, rather than the norm; and c) it seems an irrelevance since we've managed without for so long! But how much has been lost because of this…

on to gestures of arms and legs – straight, of course, and again only three levels, although a few more exciting directions may be introduced. What relation has this to *real* dancing, they may wonder? (I remember, only too well, wondering that myself; and see van Zile above.)

There are other ways of introducing notation skills, however, as a number of teachers know and employ, for example in the choreography class. One can look at principles of movement itself, what is going on, what it feels like rather than just what it looks like: centre of gravity/weight, relationship of body parts, moving through space.

Then there is motif-writing, which allows for the ideas to be jotted down or read, without the feeling of being hampered by lack of the knowledge required to get all the details (it need not be official motif-writing as such, but just quick reference symbols used in any way, as we have suggested in this book). A whole dance could be sketched in this way, giving the student a real sense of achievement and a valuable resource in their dance-making. Composers and writers have often worked like this, filling in the details later when there is time to consider, analyse and hone the necessary skills.

Perhaps the most significant issue here, however, is the fact that Labanotation, while it gives clear instructions about the mechanics of movement, is not a pictorial system. 'One is not given a picture of a final pose; instead one has to move or conceptualize the moving in order to discover the final outcome; one has to participate actively' (Youngerman 1984, p. 114). It is thus a system that can directly assist the dancer in understanding the principles underlying movement systems and choreographies, and clarify the anatomical and physiological processes of movement. This is especially significant in that it encourages dancers to discover the movement in the context of their own physique, rather than by copying an image of it, for example.

Understanding dance/embodied knowledge

And so we return to the argument about new interpretations, new performances. The celebrated dance historian Selma Jeanne Cohen (1992) interviewed the choreographer George Balanchine, who was (then, at least) against the preservation of his work; he did not want people to laugh at it in the future, he said, when it became 'old-fashioned' or irrelevant.[21] Balanchine thought that bodies would be different in the future. Having made his work on particular bodies, he did not want it to be changed by these different bodies, although he would agree to setting works for other dancers, as long as he did it himself – *or a reliable representative did.* ('I think ballet is NOW. It's about people who are NOW. It's not about what will be' [Balanchine in Cohen 1992, p. 192]).

[21] But people can be inconsistent! Balanchine also wrote the foreword to Ann Hutchinson's *Labanotation*, extolling the virtues of preserving choreographic works in notation ...'Thanks to these scores [of some of his choreographies] I am now assured that these ballets will be accurately performed in the future' (in Hutchinson 1954, p. xi).

But might not the score become the 'reliable representative' if supported by other things such as contextual research? Maybe Balanchine felt like this because he did, in fact, return to works and re-set them for different dancers, changing the choreography as he went. Perhaps, then, recognising the potential for this to happen, he worried that it would be done by others who would misread his intentions.

> If the dance world were versed in movement notation everyone would be able to examine the same non-ephemeral artifact and assess the relationship of a given performance to it and to other performances, as well as to the choreographer's original concept of what constituted the ephemeral artifact. Perhaps we would then be able to sort out the roles of choreographer, dance director, and performer – 'to know the dancer from the dance' – and evaluate each in its own right. Dance notation is certainly not *the dance* – but it can perhaps aid us in discussing with greater meaning, and in someday identifying, precisely what *is* the dance (van Zile 1985–6, p. 46).

Most people would probably agree, however, that in the process of mounting a performance, be it music, drama or dance, it is important to have a good level of contextual knowledge and understanding, and to recognise what the score/script can and cannot do. Approaching the work with respect as well as with imagination, and creativity as well as understanding, is the responsibility of the artist (and see Bonnie Rowell's essay above). The score offers insights that are invaluable in this, and is also something with which to engage creatively and imaginatively. Suzanne Youngerman again: '[n]otations are embodiments of perceptions of movement. A notation that is guided by an awareness of the ways in which movement can be conceptualized can be a source of enlightenment to anyone interested in the phenomenon of movement' (p. 118).

It will, I hope, have become clear in the course of this discussion that there are important questions to be addressed both about the proper role of notation within the discipline of dance, and the perspectives and understanding of the dance community of what that role might be. Notation needs to be able to respond to the needs of the dance community – to be something that facilitates an understanding of style in choreography and performance, offers students and scholars access to dance's history, and gives substance to the philosophical debates about dance's uniqueness. As an 'embodiment of perceptions of movement', the notated score offers the reader all these things and the opportunity to understand dance in an embodied way. But without the score, the work, the history and the experience will inevitably be lost.

Reading/Bibliography

Cohen, S.J. (1992) *Dance as a Theatre Art* (2nd edition), Hightstown, NJ, Dance Horizons.

Copeland, R. (1994) 'Reflections on revival and reconstruction', *Dance Theatre Journal*, Autumn 11/3, pp. 18–20.

Hutchinson, A. (1972) (2nd ed) (first published 1954) *Labanotation,* London, Oxford University Press.

Jordan, S. (2002) (video cassette) *Music Dances: Balanchine choreographs Stravinsky,* The George Balanchine Foundation. Distributor: Dance Books, London.

McFee, G. (1999) 'Technicality, philosophy and dance study', in G. McFee (ed.) *Dance, Education and Philosophy*, Oxford, Meyer & Meyer Sport.

Rubidge, S. (1995) 'Reconstruction and its problems', *Dance Theatre Journal*, Summer 12/1, pp. 31–33.

Taruskin, R. (1995) *Text and Act: Essays on Music and Performance*, New York, OUP.

Van Zile, J. (1985–6) 'What is dance? Implications for dance notation', *Dance Research Journal*, 17/2 & 18/1, pp. 41–47.

Yeats, W.B. (1928) *Among School Children* (poem).

Youngerman, S. (1984) 'Movement notation systems as conceptual frameworks: The Laban System', in M. Sheets-Johnstone, (ed.) *Illuminating Dance: Philosophical Explorations*, London, Toronto, Associated University Press.

2.2: Annotated Bibliography

There are many and various texts on dance notation and related subjects, and some useful contacts for further information on these and on other materials. Below are some examples of the kinds of sources available; events and training courses are listed at the end.

i. Text books, study guides and workbooks for the teaching of Labanotation

Beck, J. (1998) *Moving notation; a handbook of musical rhythm and elementary Labanotation,* Harwood Academic Publishers.

Groves, M. (1998) *Read and Dance, Books 1, 2 &3.* Choreographed and notated by Michelle Groves. Guildford, Labanotation Institute (LI).

Hutchinson, A. (1972) *Labanotation* (2nd edition), London, Oxford University Press.

Hutchinson Guest, A. (1983) *Your Move: A New Approach to the Study of Movement and Dance*, London, New York, Gordon & Breach.

__________________ (1992) *The Dancer's Glancer*, London, New York, Routledge.

Knust, A. (1979) *Dictionary of Kinetography Laban,* Plymouth, Macdonald & Evans.

Marriett, J. and Topaz, M. (1986) *Study Guide for Intermediate Labanotation*, New York, Dance Notation Bureau.

Miles, A. (1976) *The Gail Grant Dictionary of Classical Ballet Notation*, New York, Dance Notation Bureau.

_______ (1984) *Labanotation Workbook Part 1,* New York, Dance Notation Bureau.

_______ (1970) *Labanotation Workbook Part 2*, New York, Dance Notation Bureau.

Shawn, T. (1985) *16 Dances in 16 Rhythms*, London, Language of Dance Centre (LODC).

Topaz, M. (1996) *Elementary Labanotation: A Study Guide*, New York, Dance Notation Bureau.

The texts listed above are examples of those that provide a staged approach to learning notation, or are comprehensive reference sources. The Elementary and Intermediate Study Guides, for example, take you through different aspects of theory in a series of lessons. It is also possible to purchase worksheets to accompany these. For more advanced work, the *Advanced Labanotation* series of textbooks is both clear and comprehensive; the first three in the series are currently out of print, however. Check with Dance Books or the Labanotation Institute or LODC. There are also various texts that offer reading studies at different levels of complexity and focus on different dance styles (e.g. Shawn, *16 Dances in 16 Rhythms*;

also the *Read and Dance* series by Michelle Groves). These are useful in developing general dance literacy and an understanding of the process of reconstructing dance from the score and the insights that can be derived from the score about the dance, its structure and style, at an elementary level. Ann Hutchinson Guest's *Labanotation* is the notator's 'bible' – invaluable. The Knust dictionary is appropriate for the library, rather than for a personal collection! But the *Gail Grant Dictionary of Classical Ballet Notation* is a useful pocket-sized textbook, and *The Dancer's Glancer* is an excellent and handy tool in the studio.

ii. Scores of choreographies

Complete scores of professional choreographies are available for hire or reference at the **Dance Notation Bureau** in New York and the **Labanotation Institute** in Guildford. The score is normally created by the notator in collaboration with the choreographer, if this is possible, or with an appropriate representative of the choreographer. The aim is to achieve a clear documentation of the choreographer's work, which may then be used to reconstruct it. It operates similarly to a music score or play-text: i.e. there is always scope for individual interpretation. The reconstructor/_interpreter does not have to rely on other individual interpretations, as is the case if dance is recorded solely through film or video (because these media document 'a performance' of the work as interpreted by those performers/ artistic directors).

Scores available range from eighteenth-century court/social dance, through nineteenth-century ballet, to twentieth- and twenty-first-century theatre dance across a range of genres – ballet, modern dance, contemporary dance, ethnic, jazz etc. University teachers use these scores to help students develop reading skills and an understanding of issues in choreographic style and structure.

Some scores are available to buy, e.g. the Language of Dance series edited by Ann Hutchinson Guest. These include not only the Labanotation score, but also comprehensive notes on the choreography, the music, its historical and artistic context, and guidelines for reconstructing the work. Works in that series include Vaslav Nijinsky's *L'Après-midi d'un Faune*, Antony Tudor's *Soirée Musicale* and Anna Sokolow's *Ballade*. Enquire at the LI or LODC (see below) about a range of scores available to buy, including class work and studies as well as complete choreographies.

iii. Articles on the teaching, development and use of Labanotation, and issues relating to reconstruction

Some of the texts included in (i) above address the issue of teaching notation. Proceedings of the *International Conference on Kinetography Laban* regularly detail new developments in notation, as do *The Labanotator* and *Action! Recording!* (Contact the Labanotation Institute for information.)

Anon. (1989) 'Dance study supplement Part 3: Reconstruction and revival', *Dancing Times*, December.

Bartenieff, I., Hackney, P., True Jones, B., van Zile, J. and Wolz, C. (1984) 'The potential of movement analysis as a research tool: A preliminary analysis', *Dance Research Journal,* 16/1 Spring.

Copeland, R. (1994) 'Reflections on revival and reconstruction', *Dance Theatre Journal,* 11/3.

Mindlin, N. (1984) 'The process of reconstruction', *Dance Notation Journal,* 2/1 Spring.

Van Zile, J. (1985, 1986) 'What is a dance? Implications for dance notation', *Dance Research Journal* (CORD), 17/2 and 18/1, Fall and Spring.

Youngerman, S. (1984) 'Movement notation systems as conceptual frameworks: The Laban System', in M. Sheets-Johnstone (ed.) *Illuminating Dance: Philosophical Explorations,* London, Toronto, Associated University Press.

iv. Essays, articles and books using Labanotation as an illustrative or analytical or documentary tool, especially in the area of choreographic style, and comparative analysis of dances or dance styles

Chamberlain Duerden, R. (2003) *The Choreography of Antony Tudor: Focus on Four Ballets,* Madison, Teaneck, Fairleigh Dickenson University Press.

Hutchinson, Guest, A. (1981) 'The Bournonville style', *Dance Chronicle,* 4/2.

Jordan, S. (1981–2) 'Issues in Labanalysis research: Using the Humphrey scores', *Dance Research Journal* (CORD), 14/1–2.

________ (1993) '*Agon*: A musical-choreographic analysis', *Dance Research Journal,* 25/2.

________ (2000) *Moving Music: Dialogues with Music in Twentieth-century Ballet,* London, Dance Books.

Kagan, E. (1978) 'Towards the analysis of a score: A comparative study of *Three Epitaphs* by Paul Taylor and *Water Study* by Doris Humphrey'. Essays in dance research, *Dance Research Annual* (CORD), no. 9.

Topaz, M. (1988) 'Specifics of style in the works of Balanchine and Tudor', *Choreography and Dance,* vol. 1.

v. Writing on dance and sport.

This is a growing area – here is an unusual and entertaining example:

Finlay, A. (2002) *Labanotation: The Archie Gemmell Goal,* Edinburgh, pocketbooks.

Useful contacts

Dance Books (www.dancebooks.co.uk) – the best source in the UK for all publications relating to dance.

Labanotation Institute (LI@surrey.ac.uk) – for publications, teaching materials, scores for hire, notation paper, information about courses etc.

Language of Dance Centre (www.lodc.org) – for information about educational courses for all ages, publications, scores, events, links to other websites.

Dance Notation Bureau, New York (www.dancenotation.org/DNB) – for publications, teaching materials, scores to hire, information about everything connected with dance notation (specifically Labanotation, but including links to sites for other systems), links to many related sites. There are even little 'tasters' to try on-line in notation basics!

Labanwriter (www.dance.ohio-state.edu/labanwriter) – a Labanotation computer program (currently available only for Apple Macintosh). However, it is available to download free.

Calaban (www.bham.ac.uk/calaban) – a Labanotation computer program available for Windows. CD and manual £75 plus £5 p+p. Additional-use licences £25 per seat. Site-licence quotations on request. You will need a copy of AutoCAD or AutoCAD LT. For this, contact ENTEC (01462 499599). Autocad, 2006 version: £120 for educational purposes, and plus VAT for non-educational purposes. Calaban configures AutoCAD to work as a Labanotation editor.

Manchester Metropolitan University (www.mmu.ac.uk) – for Dance studies at undergraduate and postgraduate levels.

Liverpool Institute of Performing Arts (www.lipa.ac.uk) – for undergraduate programmes in Dance with Drama and Music.

Roehampton University (www.roehampton.ac.uk) – for Dance studies at undergraduate and postgraduate levels.

Coventry University (www.coventry.ac.uk) – for Dance studies at undergraduate and postgraduate levels.

University of Surrey (www.surrey.ac.uk) – for Dance studies at undergraduate and postgraduate levels. Also the home of the Labanotation Institute.

Notes on contributors

Martin Blain is Senior Lecturer in Music at Manchester Metropolitan University, where he leads a range of music programmes. His compositional output ranges from orchestral to electro-acoustic and installation pieces. As a composer he has worked on a variety of collaborative projects with choreographers, theatre directors and artists. He studied composition with Jonathan Harvey and Michael Finnissy at Sussex University and Roger Marsh at York University.

Rachel Duerden is Senior Lecturer in Dance at Manchester Metropolitan University, where she led the dance programmes from 1992 to 2005. Her book on the choreographic style of Antony Tudor was published in 2003 by Associated University Presses. Other writing includes critical essays on a variety of choreographers for *The International Dictionary of Ballet* and *50 Contemporary Choreographers*. Her research interests focus on dance–music relationships in contemporary choreography, theories of dance analysis and the role of notation in performance, choreography and analysis. She gained her PhD on the work of Antony Tudor from the University of Surrey in 1993.

Neil Fisher is a Senior Lecturer at Liverpool Institute for Performing Arts (LIPA) and a freelance dance artist/choreographer. His work habitually confounds the border between mainstream commercial work and the arts world. He has toured Britain many times and has been the recipient of several awards, including a Digital Award for *The Other Telling* and a 5* rating for his recent collaborative production at the Edinburgh Festival Fringe. He has created numerous works for youth groups, and was recently invited to Croatia to work with a team of international artists and young people creating *Secret Weapon*.

Bonnie Rowell is Principal Lecturer in Dance Studies at Roehampton University, where she researches and teaches on the dance-analysis strand of modules. Her doctorate from Roehampton in 2003 examined postmodern dance and its critical analysis, which initially prompted her interest in and continuing enthusiasm for dance and philosophy. Publications include *Dance Umbrella: The First Twenty-One Years* (2000), a celebration and overview of the Dance Umbrella Festival organisation and its continuing support for postmodern dance in the UK; and contributions to *Europe Dancing* (2000, eds Andrée Grau and Stephanie Jordan) and *Dance, Education and Philosophy* (1999, ed. Graham McFee).

Sarah Whatley is Head of Performing Arts at Coventry University and an independent performer and choreographer. She holds a PhD from the University of Surrey, Roehampton, for her work on the movement vocabulary of Siobhan Davies. Her principal research interests are dance analysis, choreographic style, dance–music relationships and pedagogical issues surrounding inclusive practices in dance techniques. She has published critical essays on issues relating to choreographic style, in particular the work of Siobhan Davies.